The
Elder Training Handbook

Testimonies about *The Elder Training Handbook*...

"Carey Green has penned great material on biblical leadership, with the focus on proper functions of a church elder. Our elder team has utilized this material in developing and training potential elders in our local church. This book a must read for every lead pastor who is venturing in raising up spiritual leadership."

- Monty Mora
Pastor, *Fountain of Life Community Church*, Pueblo, Colorado

"Going thru this curriculum has been a great opportunity to grow in my personal walk with God and to learn more history about my faith IN God."

- Aaron Hardee
Elder-candidate

"If you are looking for a simple tool to use in training up elders at your church, this is definitely worth checking out. The author has taken the system he uses at his church and put it in a book for you to just hand off to someone ready to jump in. If you don't have time to write your own customized system, I think you could easily start with this as it is. He's got tests and evaluations and explanations. It's good. Doctrinally, the author is on the conservative side of things, which means reformed theology, male eldership, etc. All good with me. My only concern with this tool is that it seems like only a few key doctrines are highlighted. Personally, I want my Elders to have an understanding of more than what this author has included in the book. I also don't know if there is an application that is given out first? It seems that the book is meant to be done alone? Is there a group component to the training? Lastly, the context of the authors church seems like it would be a bit smaller. If you are in a larger church, I don't know that would work as is. But it could be altered. But all in all, this is a good tool, especially if you are looking for something that can be totally finished in a year or so with potential elders. I'm glad I found it. I'll be suggesting it to others.

- Philip Taylor
Amazon Reviewer

A SPECIAL OFFER FOR OWNERS OF THIS BOOK

The author is available to provide customized ON-SIGHT training for those who would like a deeper dive into the contents of this book — **at a special discounted price.**

POSSIBLE SCENARIOS FOR ON-SIGHT TRAINING:

- An existing Pastor or Elder team, seeking a deeper understanding of Biblical Eldership.
- A church-wide workshop to help congregations understand the Elder role and develop their own identification, assessment, and evaluation process.
- Training for a new cohort of potential Elders (a quick-start to the process).

DETAILS OF THIS OFFER:

- Contact the author to let him know you are interested in on-sight training.
- Explain your situation and provide a couple of desired dates for a training.
- Training can be one on one or group settings (the more, the merrier)
- You will ONLY be asked to pay for the author's travel and lodging expenses.
- Additional honorarium will be left up to your prayerful discretion.

TO TAKE THE NEXT STEP

Contact the author at Carey@CareyGreen.com

The

Elder Training Handbook

Carey Green

© 2010 – Carey Green, LLC

The Elder Training Handbook
© 2010 by Carey Green, LLC
CareyGreen.com

All rights reserved. No part of this publication may be reproduced, stored in a retrieval system, or transmitted in any form by any means, electronic, mechanical, photocopy, recording, or otherwise, without prior permission of the publisher, except where provided for by USA copyright law.

Internet addresses (websites, blogs, etc.) printed in this book are offered as a resource to you. We cannot vouch for the content of these sites and the validity of the addresses for the life of this book.

Unless otherwise noted, scripture quotations are from The Holy Bible, English Standard Version® (ESV®), copyright © 2001 by Crossway, a publishing ministry of Good News Publishers. Used by permission. All rights reserved.

Printed in the United States of America

Consider these additional titles from Carey Green
https://CareyGreen.com/books

The Marriage Improvement Project (a devotional for couples)

The Dragon Slayer Chronicles (a fiction trilogy)

The Great Smizzmozzel Bash (a children's picture book)

Moving Toward God (19 discipleship lessons)

Recharge (Bible study methods and mindsets)

To my wife, friend, and ministry partner, Mindi

*The same pure & godly heart I saw for the first time
in May 1988 still entrances me today. I would not be
a teacher of God's Word, much less an Elder in the church of Jesus Christ
were it not for the grace God has given to me, through you.
Thank you, my Love, for being used of Him in such great ways in my life.*

To my children – Aaron, Melinda, Madeline, Caleb, & Faith

*Each one of you has been a blessing beyond words.
I am constantly amazed at your discernment and the
understanding each of you has of this thing we call "ministry."
Thank you for loving me and encouraging me as your Dad
and as your brother in Christ. Thank you for staying the course
in your devotion to Jesus.
I love you all!*

Contents

INTRODUCTION: Where the ETH Came From and How to Use It — i

SECTION 1: The Calling to be an Elder — 1

SECTION 2: The biblical Role of Elders — 7

SECTION 3: The External Qualifications of an Elder — 17

SECTION 4: The Internal Qualifications of an Elder — 39

SECTION 5: Essentials for the Elder: The Authority of Scripture — 55

SECTION 6: Essentials for the Elder: Basic Doctrines — 66

SECTION 7: Essentials for the Elder: Shepherding Yourself — 96

SECTION 8: Essentials for the Elder: Communicating the Gospel — 126

SECTION 9: What Next? — 134

SECTION 10: Resources — 135

INTRODUCTION:

Where the ETH Came From and How to Use It

Over the years many ideas and topics have crossed my mind as things worthy of a book – and I thought that maybe I'd write those someday. This one caught me by surprise. I never in my wildest dreams thought that I'd ever write a book on this topic. Looking back at the circumstances in which this handbook was born, it makes sense that I would do it. It happened pretty naturally, in the course of a life of ministry. It was something I needed, and the Lord provided me the means to pull it together as a gift of His grace. Let me tell you a bit of that story...

Since 1989 I've been blessed to be a leader in one form or another, in a handful of congregations of God's people. In that time my experiences and roles have been many and my love for the church has grown with each new challenge. In the midst of all that I've become more and more convinced of the vital need for well-trained, competent men — men of integrity and godly character who lead the church of Jesus Christ by example more than by virtue of their position. Without those kind of men to serve as tools in the hand of Jesus the average church member has little hope of attaining a level of maturity beyond the less-than-adequate examples he has as leaders. That's just the way it is.

In my experiences as a Pastor, I've come into a few situations where I "inherited" an Elder Team that was already in place. In some of those instances, mistakes had already been made before I got there. There hadn't been a thorough enough job done in the evaluation and training of the men who were already serving as Elders. They were all nice guys who truly loved the Lord and were willing to serve, but they hadn't been carefully assessed as to whether they fit the role and they weren't adequately equipped or effectively compelled to consider it with the seriousness both it and the church deserved.

I've stepped into other situations where I had the privilege to identify potential Elders and oversee their training from scratch. As you can probably guess, that's not an easy process. It may be why you were interested enough in this handbook to read as far as you have. By that time, I understood the need for qualified leadership in the church but was a bit hesitant to take on the kind of "equipping project" I knew was needed in order to do it right. Maybe it was my own insecurities, a perceived lack of experience, or maybe it was nothing more than fear of man. Whatever the reason, I finally got past all that and dove in. And you can be sure, I made plenty of mistakes in those early attempts. A few of those mistakes still grieve my spirit to this day.

When I started the process, I searched for resources to help me. I didn't want to re-invent something that had already been done (*Translation*: I was busy enough already!). I may have been looking in the wrong places, or maybe I didn't look long and hard enough, but I didn't find what I was looking for. There were a lot of books that taught the "head knowledge" of what Eldership is, but few that were as practical as I was wanting & needing.

So, I immersed myself in the task. I wrote up an outline... and the outline morphed into a training curriculum, and in time, into what you are reading now. This handbook is borne out of my own questions, study, frustration, and the learning that flows out of that kind of mess. It's an outgrowth of mistakes, lessons learned, and the steady hope that training men to serve as Elders *is* possible to do and that it *can* be done well.

My prayer is that any church, leadership team, or Pastor who uses this handbook will be served by it, helped to locate and train the men that the Lord Jesus is desiring to raise to the role of leadership in your church at this time. The church, as the bride of Jesus, deserves the best leadership we can provide, and I am trusting that the Spirit of God will use this handbook to help you locate those leaders and equip them to faithfully carry out His calling to shepherd His bride.

How to use this handbook

One of the main things I discovered as I began trying to identify men who might fit the role of Elder was that I didn't really *know* any of them as well as I needed to in order to assess if they were qualified to be Elders. I had initial impressions and surface opinions of them, but I needed more than that — I needed a way to see their hearts and characters. That's because the qualifications for Elders (*1 Timothy 3, Titus 1*) are about character more than anything else. That "blind spot" about the men I had in view is what shaped the design and format of this curriculum. I'll show you what I mean...

One-on-one training and assessment

As I prayerfully worked through what I perceived to be the "best practices" of identifying and training potential Elders it seemed best to go about it in a one-on-one context. Me, the Pastor, leading each potential Elder through a curriculum that teaches the biblical reality of the Elder's role. I wanted to interact with him about what he was learning and assess both his understanding and his conformity to those truths as we went along. I couldn't get around the fact that this was really the *only* way I would be able to get to know the men and to instruct them personally as they progressed.

In my case, I was the one to lead each man through the curriculum. Your situation will differ from mine. You will need to decide who should walk with your candidates through the process. It could be the Pastor, or if you have an existing Elder team, it could be individuals from that group. Either way, the person leading candidates through this curriculum needs to be a man of deep passion for the role of Elder and one who clearly understands it himself.

You may find yourself tempted to make this a "group" project — where you take 2, 3, or even 4 men through the curriculum together in a group setting. I suppose it is possible for that approach to work, but you'd have to figure out how you could have frank conversations with each of the men as you progress through the curriculum. Each one of them needs to be free to share what is **really** going on in their hearts and you need to be able to do the same regarding what you see in them as individuals.

A "no guarantees" approach

WHERE THE ETH CAME FROM AND HOW TO USE IT

I also insist (no that's not too strong of a word) that every candidate who begins this process be told, clearly and unapologetically that completing this handbook or any part of it, does **not** automatically mean he will become an Elder. You should communicate to every man who is willing to pursue this study that this process is an *exploration* as much as it is anything else. It is a means for them to understand the biblical role of Elder and compare who God has made them, to that role. It is a process of discovery — of the role and of the man being considered for the role.

One way that I applied that approach was to **repeatedly** tell the men going through this handbook something like this:

> *As you go through this handbook, there is always an "open door." That means that at any time you are free to say to me, "As I learn more about the role of Elder, I don't think it's for me." It could be a decision that it's not right for you at this time or it could be a decision that it's not a good fit — period. If either of those becomes obvious to you there is no need for embarrassment; in fact, it's the best thing for you, your family, and for the church if you figure that out sooner rather than later. But you also need to know that the "open door" swings both ways. If at any point in our times together I come to feel that you are not ready for the role of Elder, then I'm also free to tell you so and end the process.*

The reason I'm so convinced this kind of repetitive honesty is needed is because there needs to be a true evaluation of each man... a legitimate possibility that you **can** say, "no," should you need to. You won't really know every man who you consider until you get well into the process. For that reason, you should be very careful **not** to give the impression that the completion of this handbook automatically ends in becoming an Elder. *There are and can be no guarantees.*

The Holy Spirit is the one who appoints every Elder. Our evaluation and training process must allow for Him to lead in a "yes" or "no" direction at any point. Stating this attitude clearly and often enables every candidate to enter and pursue the process with a realistic expectation of the possible outcomes. And it gives you the time to *truly* assess each man.

Please, don't waffle on this... you'll be very glad you took this approach.

Regularly scheduled meetings

The way I apply the one-on-one format is to schedule weekly meetings with each man who is exploring the Elder role. This enables me to be in regular conversation with each man regarding what he is learning so that I can assess his understanding, emphasize things I feel he is not getting, and affirm him in his progress as he goes along. This enables me to see how each man is processing things and to a degree, I'm able to assess his possible fit in the Elder role. It proves to be very helpful to me and the men.

Yes, this requires a very significant investment of time — especially if you are leading more than one man through the process at once. But you **can** do it and you **should** do it if you want to find and train the right men. You are investing in their lives, in the future of your church family, and giving glory to our Savior by diligently seeking His will in the appointment of leaders for your church.

In the first session with each man, I discuss the way the handbook is laid out (which you are reading now) and the expectations of how he is to complete the work. If you want to simplify that process, there's no reason I would be averse to you giving each man a copy of this book, *including this introductory chapter*. Let them read these instructions for themselves so they can know more clearly what is expected of them and how the process will work.

I chose not to assign a specific amount of work to be completed each week. Instead, I tell each man that he should work at it diligently throughout the week, given the time constraints of his life. This allows flexibility, but also enables me to observe some very important things like the degree of motivation and self-discipline that each man has (which might also demonstrate how he might serve in the Elder role).

An intentionally prolonged process

I also find great value in taking my time in getting through the handbook with each man. In every situation to date, we have taken well over a year to complete the handbook. Beyond that, each man completed all the evaluations and assessments in the "Resource" section at the end of the handbook.

The reason I took so long was simple: *you have greater opportunity to know each man personally* over a prolonged time of study and conversation together. You will get a better feel for how he will work alongside you on a leadership team. You will be better able to assess how his personality and gifting could fit into the existing "chemistry" of your Elder team. You'll be able to see if he really understands the commitment and heart needed to serve as an Elder.

So, if I can say it again — ***don't rush the process***. Even if you desperately need leaders, it is much better to patiently complete a thorough process of Elder selection than to rush the process and wind up with the wrong men in leadership. Practically, I tell each candidate to expect that the process will take at least a year, but probably more. Again, it's important to set proper expectations up front. I also make sure to communicate the time-frame to our church family, along with my strong commitment to ensuring that we as a church do our part in properly assessing and then training those who will serve as leaders of the church.

Not only does this set everyone's expectations up front, it also teaches the congregation the seriousness and vital importance of the role of Elder. If you don't take it lightly, they will be less likely to take it lightly — and will be more willing to wait patiently for the Lord to reveal the men who should be the Elders of His church. You may want to include some congregational teaching about the role of Elder as part of your explanation of how you will be going about the process. That will help the church family value what you are doing and to understand why it is a prolonged process.

Questions & Answers

WHERE THE ETH CAME FROM AND HOW TO USE IT

This handbook contains over 260 questions for each man to consider and answer. The student should copy the given questions into a notebook and answer them honestly and fully. The questions serve two purposes:

1) They push the student to think through and apply what he's learning.
2) They allow you to hear how he is processing and applying his learning.

But don't let yourself feel tied *only* to my questions. If you've served as a church leader for any length of time my questions will likely spark memories of your own experiences. Feel free to ask additional questions, give "scenarios" that provide practical opportunities for the application of the handbook content, and challenge the student to think through "real life" situations. You'll find that type of interaction to be very beneficial.

When you complete the handbook

When an Elder-candidate completes the handbook he's really only taken the first step. In other words, He's completed the evaluation and initial training component of becoming an Elder. Beyond that, there needs to be additional assessments beyond what you as an individual have done up to this point. I chose to go through "formal" assessments of various kinds to help me, and our existing Elder team and church family get a broader perspective of each man's potential fit for the role of Elder. The process I use is outlined below.

Final assessments

Once the handbook is completed, give the student a few weeks to prepare for some "final assessments" based on the learning he's done. These take the form of a quiz covering the content of this handbook, and an oral doctrinal quiz which demonstrates if he understands the basic theological issues an Elder must firmly grasp. I leave it to you to compose your own version of the handbook quiz that covers the content of this handbook. I see no reason why you couldn't simply skim through the book, asking the candidate questions that you believe are most important for him to understand. As for the theology quiz, I have included a study guide in the "Resources" section at the end of the handbook that each man can use to prepare.

As the man you are training prepares for these quizzes, make yourself available to him for additional learning and help. If he has questions, discuss them over coffee, help him not only understand the "what" of the theological issues but also the "why," so that he has a strong basis for his belief and conviction. When it is time to administer these assessments, you can be the judge of whether trouble spots are reasons for halting the process or whether more coaching is needed and a second try is warranted.

Once the student has successfully completed those two assessments, I suggest you move forward to other types of evaluation so that you don't become a victim of your own blind spots. T far you have been the only one evaluating the man's fitness for the Elder role. You need to bring in other people to see if your impressions are right. To that end, there are 5 separate evaluations.

1. <u>A self-evaluation</u>

    The self-evaluation is an opportunity for the student to honestly assess his own fitness for the role of Elder based on the biblical qualifications for Elders. His responses to this assessment will help you to see how he perceives his own progress and learning. You may find that some men disqualify *themselves* from the process as they are faced with an honest assessment of their own readiness. I this happens, it will be a blessing to him and to the church family.

2. <u>A spousal evaluation</u>

    The spousal evaluation enables the man's wife (if he's married) to have her say about his fitness for the role. It's not uncommon for a man to feel He is more ready for the role than his wife does. If that happens, don't take it lightly. His wife may have a better feel for his readiness simply because she knows him well, warts and all. The assessment tool she will use is also based on the biblical qualifications of an Elder.

3. <u>A Pastoral evaluation</u>

    The Pastoral evaluation is likewise based on the biblical qualifications of an Elder but is not quite as formal. I chose to do this part of the process with my wife's help, over dinner with the Elder candidate and his wife. I made it clear ahead of time that our dinner was part of the process, and that I'd have some questions for the two of them regarding their feelings and thoughts about the possibility of a future Elder role. It was a great benefit for us to informally evaluate them, in a casual environment. You'll also likely find it helpful to hear your wife's impressions of the couple's readiness.

4. <u>An Elder Team evaluation</u>

    We decided to carry out this evaluation by inviting the candidate to one of our Elder meetings. We communicated clearly that we were inviting him to our meeting to "interview" him for the role of Elder. He was told to expect many questions, scenarios, and an honest discussion of the role of Elder and his interest in it. We also asked him to come with any remaining questions or concerns he might have. Having said all that, we worked hard not to make it intimidating or overbearing. The more relaxed and relational this meeting can be, the better for everyone. Once the conversation was over the Elder team discussed our impressions, the man's possible fit on our existing team, any concerns we had, and our overall conclusions. Our goal in this evaluation was to come to agreement about whether or not the man in question should be recommended to the church family for affirmation as an Elder. You should not proceed to the next step of evaluation unless the entire Elder team can honestly say that you are recommending the man to the church family.

5. <u>A congregational evaluation</u>

Before we continue with a congregational evaluation of the Elder candidate, we provide an informal opportunity for those who do not know the man to get to know him, at least on a basic level. It's very difficult for people to give a meaningful evaluation of a man they've never met. To facilitate more knowledge of the candidate we chose to host a congregational meeting that we called an "Meet N Greet." We arranged a dessert potluck (everything is better with dessert) followed by an opportunity for people to ask the candidate any questions they thought would be helpful in evaluating his fit as an Elder. We provided a list of sample questions to prime the pump, which are included in the "Resources" section at the end of the handbook. At the end of the evening, we gave each member a "Congregational Evaluation Packet" (included in the "Resources" section also). We also made those available the following Sunday for members who were not able to attend the Meet N Greet. We made sure that everyone understood the purpose of the evaluation and how to complete it properly.

Once you reach this point, you should have done your job of training and evaluation so well that there is little possibility there will be any surprises from the congregational evaluation. But that doesn't mean that there won't be any! Submitting the man to congregational evaluation enables you as church leaders to hear of any concerns that others may have about the man, since they may know him on a level that you do not. They too will be asked to evaluate the man according to the biblical qualifications for Elder, and to comment on any low scores they provide. We usually give two weeks for the congregation to prayerfully evaluate the candidate and return their assessments to the church office.

In my view, it is essential that those making this assessment include their names on their assessment. I go so far as to disqualify any that do not have a name and communicate to the congregation that we will do so. I don't only want to know the concerns people may have, I want to be able to follow up on those concerns to find out if they are real, misconceptions, hearsay, or plain old gossip. If needed, I will arrange conversations between those who have concerns and the candidate and Elder team. Everyone involved needs clarity about such things before we proceed. It is also a wonderful opportunity for Pastoral care, should the Elder and a member of the church have issues between them that need to be resolved.

Elder "installation"

Upon successfully crossing the "finish line" of all 5 evaluations you are ready to officially recognize and include the man as a part of the church leadership team. Up to this point, he has been in a process of evaluation and training, with many "open doors" along the way for the process to be stopped. It is only now that he's "in." I suggest that in keeping with the attitude of seriousness you've already communicated about the role of Elder, you center one of your public worship services around the great provision of God seen in the provision of another qualified leader for your church family. This is a good time to further instruct the church about the role and expectations of an Elder and about the church family's responsibility to honor and encourage him appropriately on an ongoing basis.

As you proceed

I know as well as anyone that mistakes can and will be made — even following careful guidelines like the ones outlined in this handbook. It's vital that you do not depend on this handbook as a guarantee or a fool-proof method for finding the right Elders. This handbook is nothing more than a resource to help you in your task of identifying and training leaders for the church. Whether you adopt this handbook as your model for Elder identification and training or use another resource, do it all in a constant spirit of prayerful dependence. The Holy Spirit must appoint Elders to His church and your diligence in assessment and training are only one of the means He will use to do so... but a very important means, nonetheless.

The journey through this handbook is not simple. It is not easy. It takes the equipping of Elders very seriously. As you talk to men about their interest in completing this handbook, be sure you communicate that fact. You want them to come into the process with their eyes wide open.

This handbook is intended to help you, as a church leader to get to know and understand how God has formed each candidate, so that you can see if he is potentially called to be an Elder. This handbook is designed to take each student deeply into the scriptures, to foster and grow a heart of passion for God's people, and to begin developing a heart of biblical wisdom which will enable them to lead God's people with care and discernment. It's not an overstatement to say that the time a man takes to complete this course may be some of the most important times of growth he experiences in his entire life. May God lead and direct as you seek to identify and train those He is calling to lead His flock, His bride, His body, the church.

the Lord's,

Carey Green, 2022

SECTION 1

The Calling To Be An Elder

And I will give you shepherds after my own heart, who will feed you with knowledge and understanding.
Jeremiah 3:15

The difference between a calling and a duty or job

We don't use the word "calling" very much in our culture anymore. There was a time when someone might say it was their "calling" to be a doctor, or policeman, or teacher. When the word "calling" is used in this way, it's intended to convey that the reason they are in that profession or doing the job they are doing is because there is a greater purpose behind their work than simply their desires and interests. They likely even feel a sense that they are "supposed" to be doing the work they are doing.

On the other hand, when we speak of a job or duty, we usually mean something less significant or less vital than a calling. It's what we do because we have to, to put food on the table and pay the bills. A job may be identical to a calling in terms of what is done, but that doesn't automatically make it a calling. *A calling is from God.*

There is a sense in which every Christian has a calling in a variety of areas. We are to live in ways that honor God, we are to make disciples, we are to embrace and speak God's truth. But the "calling" to be an Elder, is not one that every man will receive. It is a commission from God Himself to be a part of a team of men who will lead their local church family into greater maturity, greater commitment to Jesus, and greater effectiveness in carrying out His mission for their local church family.

Let's look at a scriptural example of this kind of calling...

The Lord Calls Jeremiah – Jeremiah 1:5-10

Q&A

1. According to this account, WHEN did God appoint Jeremiah to the work He had for him to do?

   Before born!

2. What does that tell you about God's purposes? Are they random? Are they in response to things? Are they spontaneous? *They are planned by God*

3. What was Jeremiah's response? *I am too young. Excuses*

4. Is there any way in which you feel hesitant or incapable (like Jeremiah) when you consider that God may be calling you to the role of Elder? Be honest...

5. What did God do for Jeremiah? Do you think He would do this for you if you are called to be an Elder? *Put His words in his mouth & empowered Him*

6. If you are called to be an Elder, who has determined that purpose for you? *God!*

7. If you were to become an Elder, where would your strength need to be? In other words, who is it that accomplishes the work of an Elder – you, or someone else? *God!*

Examining your own calling

The saying is trustworthy: If anyone aspires to the office of overseer, he desires a noble task. - **1 Timothy 3:1**

According to Paul's words to Timothy, anyone who desires to serve as an Elder desires a noble task. But it's important to know the "why" behind your desire to serve as an Elder. Taking the time to deeply probe and answer that question can help you to determine if God is truly calling you to this important task or not. In this section we'll examine some scriptures that may help in this process...

Peter's Words to Elders – 1 Peter 5:1-4

Verse 1 shows us that Peter was appealing to these men to consider the proper way to carry out their role as Elders. He does so on the basis of three things... 1) He too was an Elder, so he knew what he was talking about, 2) He was an eye-witness of the sufferings of Jesus, so he knew firsthand the price Jesus paid to establish the church, and 3) He saw himself as one who would share in the glory God has in store for all believers.

Q&A

8. Does it make a difference in how you read Peters words, knowing that he was himself an Elder of God's church? *yes*

9. When you consider what it took for Jesus to establish the church, how does that impact the way you look at the responsibilities and role of an Elder? *He paid so much – I can not!!*

THE CALLING TO BE AN ELDER

10. Thinking that you will one day stand before Christ, are you motivated to take on this role and serve well, or does it bring a sense of hesitance about becoming an Elder at all? *Motivated*

11. Peter's first instruction about being an Elder is to "shepherd the flock that is under your care." Describe what it means to you to be a shepherd of other people. *Responsible & Care for them.*

12. How does it impact you to know that should you become an Elder, people for whom Jesus died will be "under your care?" *They are valuable to Jesus -- I must care for them.*

13. As you consider these things, do you sense a deep desire to *be* a shepherd? Do you sense a deep desire *to care* for Christ's church, His bride? *Yes*

14. Peter also says that Elders are to serve "*not because you must, but because you are willing, as God wants you to be.*" Is there any sense in which you are feeling an obligation to serve as an Elder? *I am called!*

15. If so, is it a healthy sense of obligation because God's calling is behind it, or is it something else? *God's Calling!*

16. Peter cautions against greed on the part of Elders. It may seem an awkward question to be asked, but is there any sense in which you are anticipating that being an Elder will profit you personally? *No! It will cost me!*

17. In contrast to greed, Elders are told that they must be "*eager to serve.*" Being an Elder is a very humbling and self-sacrificial task. Have you considered that as an Elder you will need to be "eager" to help meet the needs of others, walk through their struggles with them, and guide them into a greater knowledge of and relationship with Jesus? Can you truly say that you are "eager" to fill those shoes? *Yes!*

18. Can you give some examples of how an Elder might "*lord it over*" others in the way Peter describes? Why is this inappropriate? *Be demanding - Legalistic rather than a purveyor of Grace!*

19. Instead of being dominant, Elders are to be good examples to the flock under their care – a godly man they can look up to and respect. Realistically, what are your strengths in this arena (don't be afraid of bragging, instead give God credit for what He's done in you)? *Able to teach & preach - Care for lost!*

20. What are your areas of weakness in this area? Do you have plans to address them? *Not a people person - Study God's Grace & Help*

Genuine care, willingness, eagerness to serve others, and personal example are vital to the role of Elder. Hopefully this series of questions, based on Peter's heart for the church and for Elders has helped you to examine your own heart. You'll have opportunity at the end of this section to put your self-evaluation on paper, so you can look it over and spend time before the Lord praying about whether He is issuing you a calling to be an Elder.

Considering the timing/readiness issue

It is not uncommon for God's calling to be on a person's life, but for a later time. There are times when you think you are ready, but God doesn't, even though His calling is clearly upon you to be heading in the direction you are. In situations like this He will reveal His desires for you, either through times in the word and prayer where He clearly speaks to you about your readiness, or through friends, a sermon, a song, circumstances, or something else. Remain open to what He may be saying. His timing is of the greatest importance and will work out for the best — for you, your family, and for the church.

Another aspect of timing has to do with your "pace of life." An Elder's responsibilities are not like a hobby or a side-job. They are of the utmost importance. Your consistent and committed involvement will require time — and in certain seasons, lots of it. It is vitally important that you take the time during the exercises at the end of this section to clearly and honestly evaluate your own ***availability***. Some things to consider are the number of hours you work per week (including commute time), the amount of time required for family events (soccer, music recitals, etc.), the time needed to maintain a healthy and exemplary relationship with your wife and children, the energy and time required to keep your relationship with the Lord up to date and vibrant, and your "stage" of life (retired, new career, young family, etc.). Considering each area individually may enable you to see your current commitments more realistically and get a better feel for what your life's "pace" is really like.

Family life, outside events, work, and other responsibilities are areas in which we Christians demonstrate the life of Christ in our daily lives. They are a very important aspect of our Christian witness and are not to be taken lightly. However, if the pace of your life is such that the combination of these things might regularly deter you from consistently fulfilling the responsibilities of Elder, then the time for your calling to be fulfilled may yet be in the future. As you consider the time and energy that your life currently requires, seriously consider whether you will be able to fulfill the important, life-giving responsibilities of a shepherd of Jesus' church.

The importance of your wife's support

Scripture calls men, not women to serve as Elders. However, there are obvious ways in which an Elder's wife contributes to the success of his role. There will be situations where women of the church need a female perspective and presence and the Elder's wife is the natural person to provide that. As well, there will be many situations where the Elders will actively seek the counsel and understanding of their wives regarding decisions they need to make on behalf of the church family. These are only some of the many scenarios where it is imperative that the heart of an Elder's wife, in terms of love and commitment to the Lord and ministry to other people, needs to mirror those of her husband.

Imagine the impact if an Elder's wife did not share his desire to shepherd God's people.

THE CALLING TO BE AN ELDER

Emergency needs among the church family might become areas of resentment for the wife. She could begin to feel that the needs of their family are not as important to her husband as the needs of the church family. He would not have the much-needed and vitally important resource of a godly, female perspective from which to gain additional wisdom for his role. His own home may suffer from lack of a united, Spirit-filled effort in directing their family toward God's glory and will in all things. There is a sense in which one could say that an Elder's wife must have a calling to be the supportive partner and helper to her Elder-husband that God intends for her to be. A man considering the role and calling of Elder must take time to honestly evaluate this issue alongside his wife.

With all that said, a word of clarification may be in order. In no way should you conclude that the Elder's family is in fact to come second to the church family and church business. Quite the opposite is true. An Elder cannot be the example scripture calls him to be if his own family is not one of his highest priorities. A man is disqualified from leadership if the condition of his own household becomes one of disorder or discord, or if those under his fatherly care turn from the Christian faith. *The family must come first.*

SELF-EVALUATION EXERCISES

The questions and exercises to follow are for your benefit, to allow you time to think through the issues covered in this section. Take your time, answer honestly and prayerfully, and do your best to respond thoughtfully and carefully.

- Do you have a sense that God is calling YOU to serve in the role of Elder? If so, what is that calling based upon?

- Is your walk with the Lord of a high enough quality that you can feel confident that any "sense" you have from the Lord about this issue is genuinely from Him? Explain...

- Explain any significant or nagging sense in which you feel you are **not** ready.

- What is your estimation of your "desire" to serve as an Elder? Is it a pure desire to serve or is it colored by something else? Explain...

- Concerning the issue of "personal example," none of us is perfect. Nevertheless, the role of Elder is one of example. With that in mind, are there any ways in which you believe you are not ready to be an Elder because of issues having to do with your ability to be a good example? Please explain...

- How would you characterize your "pace of life" at this point? Do you have room in your normal schedule to take on the serious responsibilities of an Elder? If not, do you believe that there are chunks of time you should clear out so that you could? Please explain...

CAREY GREEN

- What is your wife's attitude about this step? Is she spiritually ready for you to take on this responsibility?

- Do you see your wife being able to help shepherd others alongside you? Please explain...

- What leadership steps do you regularly take to ensure that your family is growing in knowledge and application of the Word of God?

- Is there any reason the condition or state of your family gives you reason to pause as you consider becoming an Elder? If so, please explain...

- Describe your own personal walk with the Lord. Include things such as your attitude and practice concerning the scriptures, prayer, journaling, etc.

> **SCRIPTURE MEMORIZATION**
> *So I exhort the elders among you, as a fellow elder and a witness of the sufferings of Christ, as well as a partaker in the glory that is going to be revealed: shepherd the flock of God that is among you, exercising oversight, not under compulsion, but willingly, as God would have you; not for shameful gain, but eagerly; not domineering over those in your charge, but being examples to the flock. And when the chief Shepherd appears, you will receive the unfading crown of glory.*
> **1 Peter 5:1-4**

SECTION 2

The Biblical Role Of Elders

shepherd the flock of God that is among you, exercising oversight, not under compulsion, but willingly, as God would have you...
1 Peter 5:2

Elders as examples

A good example is hugely important. Few of us would think it helpful to faithfully attend aerobics classes led by a 500 pound instructor. We wouldn't take a seminar on "How to Make Your First $1 million" from a guy who lives in a cardboard box on the street. Why? Because they don't practice what they preach. Example matters!

As you continue to contemplate the role of Elder for yourself, you need to know that one of the primary ways that you will benefit the people under your care is by living out the life that you are encouraging them toward. Of course, no Elder will be perfect, but every Elder should be consistently gaining ground in integrity, character, and spiritual maturity... all which translate into a life worth following. There is no substitute for a leader who lives out what he is leading others to do.

In every organization, but especially the church, every significant opportunity for growth will rise or fall on leadership. If the Elders of a church are men who are demonstrating personal growth and integrity, then the church will naturally move in that direction under their leadership. But if the Elders are men who are spiritually inconsistent, prideful, and self-interested, then the church will flounder at best and shrivel up and die at worst.

For a church Elder, one of the first and most important areas where consistency must a characteristic of his life is in his own relationship with Jesus. An Elder has to recognize the truth that his own spiritual health is dependent on his connection with Jesus at any given moment. Godliness only comes through **connection with** God. Holiness only comes through contact with the One who is holy. Righteousness only comes from the King of righteousness. As Elders, we need to make one of our top priorities our own personal relationship with God the Father, through our Lord Jesus. In this way we will be living out our own healthy and vibrant walk with the Lord that will enable us to be a daily example of Christian commitment for those we lead.

Let's look at some scriptures...

<u>Paul's example – 1 Corinthians 11:1, Philippians 3:17</u>

Q & A

21. Re-write Paul's instruction in these verses in your own words.

22. Who was Paul following? What do you think was involved in that?

23. In our day, it might sound a bit arrogant to tell others to imitate you. How could Paul have the guts to say something like this?

24. Do you think that an Elder in your church should be able to say the same sort of thing? Explain?

25. Do you feel that you are personally able to make this kind of statement to those who are currently under your care (your family)? If not, what will it take to get there?

Paul's instructions to church leaders – 1 Timothy 4:12-16 / Titus 2:7-8

Q & A

26. While it is true that many people may "look down on" their leaders for various reasons (in Timothy's case, he was young), what does Paul say is the solution to that problem?

27. Notice the areas in which Paul tells Timothy to be an example. Write out your thoughts about what is involved in being an example in each of those areas.
    - Speech
    - Life
    - Love
    - Faith
    - Purity

29. In the church, why is the life of an Elder so important as an example?

30. What begins to happen in the church when the members begin to see evidence of a "bad example" in their leaders?

31. How do you feel about yourself as an example of a Christian man & leader? Are there any areas of weakness or need where you'd like specific help?

Elders as Overseers

One of the words commonly translated as "Elder" in the New Testament (the Greek word, *Episkopos*) is most literally rendered "Overseer." We don't use the word "Overseer" much anymore. It's been replaced by words like "manager," "supervisor," and "boss." But it's a word that we need to resurrect in the church and use more often. It's a word that defines itself the minute you say it. Take a look at what I mean...

Over-seer: One who oversees.

What the Overseer oversees has to do with the context in which he's working. In our case, the church is the context where an Overseer does his work. Functioning as an Overseer means more than simply observing what is happening. That's an observer. An Overseer is one who observes and then acts according to the needs that he sees. In the church, Overseers are charged by Jesus to prayerfully guide, direct, and care for His church.

Imagine a business whose CEO was regularly detached from the day to day operations of the business. Imagine that he spent very little time thinking about the company's progress and health and hardly ever worked to train and encourage the employees or develop and improve the products. What do you think would happen to that business? It's only a matter of time until that company is filing bankruptcy — all because of a lack of good OVERSIGHT. Bad management will kill any organization, including the church.

When the church does not have spiritually mature, diligent oversight, it's only a matter of time until it loses its focus and becomes self-absorbed and ineffective in the world. The health, direction, and mission of the church is to be regularly evaluated and considered by a group of mature, godly men — the Elders, or Overseers. But the church is different from a business in that the main realm of oversight is not products, but people...

Paul's instruction to a group of Overseers – Acts 20:28

Q & A

32. Paul is speaking to the Elders of the church at Ephesus for the last time. Reading a bit more before and after, you can see it's a very emotional scene. Paul uses the words "keep watch" to describe part of their duties. How do those words relate to the idea of being an Overseer?

33. What are the two things Paul says that Elders are to keep watch over?

34. What ways can you think of in which an Elder can or should keep watch over himself and /or the other Elders?

35. What are some of the primary areas in which an Elder should be keeping watch over the church?

36. Paul says that it is the Holy Spirit who has made each Elder an Overseer of the church. Write down your thoughts about the honor and importance of that appointment.

37. Notice verse 30. Paul says that wolves may rise up to attack the flock... and from a very unexpected place. What place is it?

38. How can Overseers do their best to prevent this sort of thing from happening?

Elders as doctrinal guardians

In Paul's instructions to the Ephesian Elders that we just considered, he says that men will arise who *"distort the truth."* It is part of the Overseer's job to carefully consider what is being taught to the church under his care. Teaching is vitally important and requires a united effort among the Elder team to make sure that wrong teachings can be avoided or counteracted appropriately if they do arise.

But underneath that is the assumption that the Overseers can spot false teaching when it shows up. That means that Elders need to be well-versed in the basic teachings about God, salvation, and eternity. It is imperative that every Elder is continually immersing himself in the word of God – learning, growing, and preparing for the day when he may be called upon to serve the church as a guardian of the truth.

Q & A

39. Is the idea of serving as a "doctrinal guardian" of the church intimidating to you? If so, why do you think it is?

40. What areas of biblical knowledge do you feel you know well? What areas do you feel you need a better grasp of?

41. Two primary areas that Elders need to understand thoroughly are the Doctrine of the Trinity and the Doctrine of Salvation. Why do you think these two are so fundamental?

Elders as Shepherds

Paul also told the Ephesian Elders that they are to *"be shepherds of the church of God."* The imagery he is using to help them understand their role is unmistakable. Just as the shepherd is tasked with leading the flock, providing the sheep food and protection, and ensuring their overall well-being, so is the role of the Overseer/Elder. There will be sheep of all kinds in the flock of the church at any given time. Some are weak, others sick, while still others are distressed. It is the shepherd's job to wisely shepherd each one.

The condition of the flock – Proverbs 27:23-24

THE BIBLICAL ROLE OF ELDERS

Q & A

42. As Elders we can glean some helpful principles from the ideas in these verses. What do you see as the main point of the passage?

43. Part of knowing the condition of the flock has to do with assessing their spiritual health and maturity. Do you have any ideas as to how an Elder team can do that effectively in regard to the people in the church?

One size does NOT fit all – 1 Thessalonians 5:12-14

Q & A

44. In this passage, Paul instructs the entire church in how to care for one another, but it holds some valuable insights for the Elder. He does mention 4 specific types of people who may be within the church. What are the 4 types of people he lists?

45. Does Paul suggest the same type of ministry response toward each of these kinds of people? What reasons do you think could be behind his instruction?

46. Do you think it's accurate for us to say that Paul is advocating a careful assessment of those in the church so that their particular needs can be addressed? Why or why not?

47. There are two types of ministry Paul lists that are appropriate for everyone. What are they?

48. Why do we need to strive for "peace" with everyone? What type of peace do you think he's talking about?

49. Does this mean that Christians (Elders) should sweep things under the rug in order to maintain peace? Give some ideas you might have about how Elders can strive to have peace with others while at the same time upholding standards of truth and right behavior?

50. Why do you think Paul prescribed patience toward everyone?

The importance of godly wisdom

No Elder, no matter how long he has been a Christian, will be able to serve appropriately and adequately in his role as Overseer if he does not have a significant dose of godly wisdom. It only takes a few quick trips into the book of Proverbs to realize that God puts a premium on wisdom and encourages it for His people. Doesn't it make sense that a leader should especially seek out wisdom?

The promise of wisdom – James 1:5

Q & A

51. The first words James records here are vital... "If any of you **lacks** wisdom..." Why do you think it's important to acknowledge our lack of wisdom?

52. Once we know our need for wisdom, what are we to do about it?

53. When James tells us that God gives generously, what is it that He gives?

I'd encourage you to make a daily request for God's wisdom a part of your daily prayers. You'll be amazed at how God answers!

Four characteristics of godly wisdom – Proverbs 1:1-7

Teachability

Q & A

54. Verse 5 and verse 7 contrast differing attitudes between a wise person and a foolish person. What is the attitude of a wise person, especially in regard to wisdom? What is the attitude of a foolish person?

55. It appears from verse 7 that a foolish person thinks they already have enough wisdom, while a wise person wants to gain more wisdom. Are you eager to gain more wisdom, or do you think you're pretty wise already?

56. The wise person maintains an attitude of teachability. They want to know their weaknesses so that they can learn to overcome them with God's help. How should this kind of humility be demonstrated in an Elder Team?

57. If even the wise need to *"add to their learning,"* we can assume that the process of learning wisdom will be ongoing. How can Elder Teams make sure they are individually and corporately moving in this direction?

58. If an Elder Team is truly teachable, what type of leadership do you think they will exhibit? Arrogant? Domineering? Wishy-washy? Something else?

Discernment

Q & A

59. Define what it means to be "discerning?" What does verse 5 say about it?

60. Literally, discernment means "sorting out" the information we have received. We have to learn to categorize things as true or untrue, consistent or inconsistent with God's values, or simply inappropriate. Do you find yourself able to do this well, or is it a struggle for you?

61. What role does knowledge of the scriptures play in discernment?

62. What handicaps might you experience in discernment if you don't know the scriptures well?

63. What role do you think the Elder Team as a group could play in discerning the best decisions to take on behalf of the church?

Action

Q&A

64. Verse 3 lists three outcomes of a wise life. List them and comment on what you understand each one to be.

65. Someone once said that knowledge is knowing the right thing to do, and wisdom is doing it. What do you think of that statement?

66. Once you arrive at what you believe to be a wise decision, is it always easy to do the right thing? With this in mind, what role does discipline play in the application of wisdom?

Fear of the Lord

Q&A

67. Proverbs 1:7 shows us a very important distinction between godly wisdom and other so-called wisdom. godly wisdom has a very clear foundation - "*the fear of the Lord.*" Is this simply respect, or is it something more? Write your thoughts about it.
68. The Hebrew word used here literally means "fear." It is the fear we read about in Exodus 20:18-21, Luke 5:8, and Isaiah 6:1-7. Take time to read those passages and then share any additional thoughts you have about the meaning of the phrase "*the fear of the Lord.*"

69. With all of this in mind, why do you think, "*the fear of the Lord is the beginning of wisdom?*"

70. When we see ourselves accurately in light of who God really is, it should produce a very healthy fear, and therefore the beginning of a humble and teachable heart of wisdom. Please share any further thoughts you have.

WRITTEN QUIZ

In the following questions, do your best to answer without reviewing this section. If you have trouble recalling the information, don't worry – you'll discuss your answers with your mentor!

- What does the term "Overseer" mean in regard to an Elder? What is he overseeing and why is his role important?

- List some of the reasons that an Elder needs to be a good example to those under his care.

- What does it mean that an Elder is to "shepherd" those under his care?

- How is an Elder to be a "doctrinal guardian" of the church? What is required in order for him to do this aspect of his job well?

SELF-EVALUATION EXERCISES

In light of the Elder's responsibilities as an example, Overseer, shepherd, and doctrinal guardian, please answer the following questions to help you evaluate yourself in each of those areas.

In regard to being an example to the flock in speech, life, love, faith, and purity – complete the following scales:

SPEECH
(the overall quality, character, and appropriateness of your language)

LIFE
(the overall quality, character, and appropriateness of your life and lifestyle)

THE BIBLICAL ROLE OF ELDERS

LOVE
(the genuine love and concern you show to others, inside and outside your family)

FAITH
(the overall degree of spiritual consistency and trust you demonstrate in your life)

PURITY
(the degree of uprightness and right motives typical of your life)

In regard to serving as an Overseer, shepherd, and doctrinal guardian of the flock of God, please complete the following evaluations:

- I deeply care for the spiritual condition of others, both inside and outside my family.

- I deeply desire to provide others with spiritual encouragement and support so they can grow to be more like Christ.

- It is very important to me to provide spiritual protection for others against false doctrine.

- On this question, put "yes" in the blanks of the false teachings you could defend against and "no" in the blanks of those you could not. If you do not know what a particular teaching is, put "no" in that blank. (Don't sweat it, I need a refresher on all of these too!)

_____ Jehovah's Witness
_____ Mormonism
_____ Roman Catholicism
_____ Open Theology
_____ Arianism
_____ Modalism

_____ Polytheism
_____ Word of Faith theology
_____ Islam
_____ Pantheism
_____ good works salvation
_____ prosperity gospel

SCRIPTURE MEMORIZATION
Let no one despise you for your youth, but set the believers an example in speech, in conduct, in love, in faith, in purity.
1 Timothy 4:12

SECTION 3

The External Qualifications Of An Elder

With any responsibility, from a job to a leadership position in a group or club, there are qualifications that must be met if you want to serve in that role. The same is true of the role of Elder. These qualifications, as stated in the scriptures, set a very high biblical standard for the life and character of any man who desires to serve God's church as one of its leaders. While no man will perfectly meet these criteria they serve as a barometer through which the church can determine if the direction and pattern of a man's life fits him for the role of Elder.

In this and the following section, you will be walking carefully through the biblical descriptions of these qualifications. The aim is to have a clear understanding of each of them, and to consider your own life in light of their demands. Let's dive in...

Husband of one wife – 1 Timothy 3:2

At first glance, it may appear that few men in the modern world would have a problem in meeting this requirement. After all, only extreme religious sects, or primitive cultures believe in or practice having more than one wife in our day. But that understanding of this text misses its true meaning. Even in the day when this was written, there were not many who supported or encouraged having multiple wives, so it's pretty unlikely that Paul intends us to think that he's talking about an Elder having only one wife. The emphasis Paul is making has to do with a man's faithfulness to his wife.

Some biblical scholars have suggested that a more accurate translation of this phrase is that the Elder must be a "one woman man." Being a "one woman man" means that the Elder is a man who has made a solemn commitment before God, and to his spouse, that he will be faithful to his marriage covenant. Some of the practical things this means are:

1. Flirting with other women is entirely inappropriate. When you flirt with a woman who is not your wife, you are opening the door to a room that a faithfully married man can never go into. To hint at doing so through flirting is not only foolish, but very disrespectful and even sinful toward your wife.
2. Relationships with women that move beyond basic friendship are violations of the sacred covenant of marriage.
3. Use of sexually explicit materials such as pornographic movies, novels, magazines, and websites are in clear opposition to the "one woman man" principle. They stir up lust aimed toward other women... and erode the fabric of your marriage commitment.

4. Even some of the more mainstream movies depict scenes, behaviors, and attitudes that lead your thoughts away from this "one woman man" principle by inciting lust. Of course, it's fictional, but as Pastor and author John Piper says, *"that lady is really naked, and I am really watching."*[1] Its' best for Elders to avoid such forms of entertainment altogether in order to maintain this "one woman man" principle.

In order to maintain integrity in this area, each Elder must do his utmost to protect himself from the images, situations, and stimulations that are aimed at destroying his commitment to being a "one woman man." The sexual relationship that a man shares with his wife is to be exclusive to her. Not only does this honor the commitment that he made when he married her, it also honors *her* by demonstrating the exclusivity of his love and commitment *to* her.

But there's more here that we should carefully consider. Sexuality is one of the many danger zones for men in general. In our day adultery is common and comments of a sexual nature are everywhere. It's even crept into the church. Most but not all instances where a Pastor or church leader is disgraced in our day, it has to do with sex. In light of that, there is another passage that sheds light on this issue for us...

Let marriage be held in honor among all, and let the marriage bed be undefiled, for God will judge the sexually immoral and adulterous. - **Hebrews 13:4**

It's clear from this verse that the words "marriage" and "the marriage bed" are speaking of the sexual relationship between a man and his wife. What is it that this scripture is saying to us about that relationship? First, marriage and in particular the sexual aspects of the marriage relationship are to be held "*in honor.*" When we think of something honorably, we think well of it, we hold it in high esteem. Sex within marriage is to be valued and esteemed very highly. We are to treasure the sexual relationship God has given us with our wives and see to it that our attitude about it is one of care and protection. Let's take a few moments to think this through...

Remember, the writer is talking about sexual relationships within *marriage*. Let that sink in. Marriage: the spiritual and physical union of one man and one woman. For a husband and wife, their sexual relationship is one of the most intimate and private acts in which they engage together. And it is perhaps the most powerful symbol of the unity they share under God as husband and wife. That unity, that intimacy, that privacy is part of the sacred "honor" of marriage. It's a relationship that the husband and wife share with nobody else. It's a union of two people - no more. What does this mean practically?

Any man, but especially one who desires to be an Elder in the church, should do his utmost to keep the sexual aspects of his marriage private, out of reverence and care for the precious and intimate gift that it is. He should examine his speech to make sure that his comments are never of a suggestive or sexual nature. When a man makes those kinds of comments, he is causing everyone who hears him to think on a sexual level, to move their focus to an area that is intended by God to be intimate and private between a man and his wife. When sexual innuendo or joking is part of a man's conversation, he is not only raising a private subject

---

[1] http://www.desiringgod.org/resource-library/taste-see-articles/why-i-dont-have-a-television-and-rarely-go-to-movies

THE EXTERNAL QUALIFICATIONS OF AN ELDER

to the level of public attention, he is also lessening the honor and intimacy of the sexual union God has given him with his wife. Additionally, if the man is an Elder, he is diminishing his own respect as an Elder, in the eyes of those who overhear him.

Let's flesh it out with a practical scenario that will illustrate this important point. Imagine yourself as a fairly new attender at a church. You and your family have enjoyed the teaching, worship, Sunday school classes, and the fellowship of the church family. It is a very warm and inviting place. The Pastor and his wife invite you to their house for dinner, along with some of the other Elders in the church and you are eager to attend so that you can get to know the leadership of the church.

During the dinner conversation the Pastor and one of the Elders who is seated near you, begin lightheartedly joking together, and a few mild, but sexually-oriented comments are included. They laugh and joke together, clearly not thinking that anything "wrong" is being said. What sort of impression would that conversation give you about those men? Do you see them as Christ-like leaders who seem trustworthy and "above reproach?" Or do you to feel that the church's leaders may be too worldly-minded, or perhaps unreliable as spiritual leaders?

An Elder is to be a shepherd to the people of the church. He is to guide them into life-giving, spiritually vibrant directions in their actions and in their thoughts. He is to lead them to God, to show them His glory and majesty, to magnify His marvelous grace and love shown in Christ's sacrifice on the cross. He is to encourage them and speak to them in ways that cause them to become more firmly grounded in their faith and ready to endure hardship for Jesus' sake if necessary. He is to point them toward God's will for their lives - over and over again.

With all of this in mind, does it seem appropriate for an Elder to steer any non-teaching type of conversation with those in his flock toward a sexual direction? Paul answers these questions best when he writes...

> *But sexual immorality and all impurity or covetousness must not even be named among you, as is proper among saints. Let there be no filthiness nor foolish talk nor crude joking, which are out of place, but instead let there be thanksgiving. -* ***Ephesians 5:3-4***

The New International Version says, "*But among you there must not be even a **hint** of sexual immorality*" Not even a hint. Think about that for a moment... the person observing your life is the one who will get the "hint" as to whether there is any sexual immorality present. What does that mean practically? It means that you will likely have to go overboard to make sure that there is nothing in your life that others could possibly construe to be a hint of immorality. That is a very high standard – one that is consistent with the holiness of the God we serve.

Here we again see a theme that will recur over and over throughout this handbook. Elders are to be examples to the flock in a way that is above reproach. Consider this in contrast to the world in which we live. With very few exceptions, television shows, movies, and even the songs of our day treat sex as a casual, voyeuristic act that is not worthy of respect or honor. Celebrities and public figures show little discretion when it comes to sexual things. The honorable intimacy and high value of the sexual relationship has been cheapened to the level of a sit-com punch line.

Paul is telling us that even though these things may be characteristic of the world we live in, they *must not* be characteristic of the church – and that difference must begin with its leaders. Elders cannot be like those men in the world who joke and tease about sexual things, and in so doing drag the beauty, glory and intimacy of the marriage bed out into the view of a sneering, lust-saturated world. To do so is to show that we are really not so different from the world... and that Jesus has made little difference in our lives.

The church cannot afford to send that kind of message. We must make sure that there is no question in the minds of those we lead, that we are men of integrity when it comes to sex and sexually oriented things. Any comments of a sexual nature should be reserved for times of intimacy between a husband and his wife, or for times of biblical teaching regarding the proper role and practice of sex.

Q & A

71. Explain why Paul requires Elders to be "one woman" men?

72. What are some of the specific areas of a man's behavior and mindset where this principle should be applied?

73. Explain why it is so important that Elders are careful to keep their conversation free from sexual innuendo.

74. Why do you think Paul makes a point of saying "*not even a hint*" of sexual immorality should be among believers?

75. What would be the effect on the church and the outside world if Elders were NOT faithful in sexual matters?

76. Explain how the Elder's integrity in sexual areas supports and honors the calling of the church to make disciples.

Children are believers – Titus 1:6

What difference does it make if an Elder of the church has children who are not faithful to the Lord? The answer may seem pretty obvious, but to make sure you see it, let's walk through the implications. The mission of the church, and those who are within the church, is to make disciples, followers of Jesus. Every man needs to know how to lead his first disciples – his children – into initial *and* ongoing faith in Jesus Christ. This is especially true of Elders.

An Elder's family is made up of the people who, out of all the people in the world, love, honor, and respect him the most. They are the people who are most likely to listen to his wise counsel. They are the people he should care about more than any others. Therefore, his family should be one of the areas where he is most naturally eager to encourage and facilitate spiritual fruit. You might say that the faith or lack of faith seen in an Elder's children, serves to show whether he is able to make disciples at all.

THE EXTERNAL QUALIFICATIONS OF AN ELDER

Having said that, let me make this qualification... you cannot **make** your children trust in Christ, which is the work of the Spirit of God Many a parent has done their children great harm by pressuring their kids to "say the prayer" to accept Christ. That attitude shows that the parent has a ***huge*** misunderstanding of how salvation happens in the first place.

It is a sovereign act of Almighty God when a person comes to faith in Christ. It is an awakening of the dead (*Ephesians 2:5*), a blowing of the wind of the Spirit (*John 3:5-8*) that brings about faith. We don't produce that, in ourselves, *or* in our children. We can facilitate it, encourage hearts toward it, teach about it, and proclaim it as a necessity. But we don't make it happen.

Some questions naturally arise as we consider this requirement for Elders. *"What about children who are too young to understand their need for Christ?"* Naturally, issues like this must be taken into account with grace and discernment. No parent should ever demand or insist on more than their children are able to handle. It's not only harsh to do so but is also unloving.

But a caution is in order. I've heard people characterize an intentional approach to discipling our children as "pushing them" into the faith. They say that we should allow our children to "make their own choices" when it comes to matters of faith. While it is true, as said before, that we cannot *cause* our children to believe in Christ (and should not try to do so), that does not mean that we are to be unintentional in guiding our children in their spiritual beliefs and life.

Think about it: We intentionally teach and guide our children in ***all other*** aspects of their developing lives – relationships, manners, hygiene, sports, school, work, etc. We do so according to what we, as their parents, believe is best for them. That's the job of a parent, isn't it? Why should spiritual understanding and growth, which is of much greater importance than anything else, be deemed off limits? Why would we want to leave our children *all to themselves* in figuring out something of such eternal significance?

As responsible and diligent parents it is our ***duty*** to guide our children – the very first disciples the Lord entrusts to us – into a growing understanding of saving faith in Christ. Our children love and trust us above all others, and we should not let them down by failing to lead them into spiritual truth. Don't make the mistake of waiting for your children to show spiritual interest on their own. Begin when they are very young to talk of Jesus, salvation, worship, God's goodness, etc.

But be careful of another danger – hypocrisy. If you talk a loud Christian talk, but are not living it out passionately yourself, your kids will see right through it. They need to see that what you are teaching them is truly important to you. They need to see you growing in humility, wisdom, patience, and the other fruit of the Spirit. Jesus needs to be the constant conversation of your home, because He is the constant companion of your heart. Don't make the mistake of thinking that talking about Jesus, without making Him real in your own life will effectively lead your children to Christ. It won't. In fact, it will probably do exactly the opposite.

Q & A

77. In 2004, a Barna Group study indicated "that nearly half of all Americans who accept Jesus Christ as their Savior do so before reaching the age of 13 (43%), and that two out of three born again Christians (64%) made that commitment to Christ before their

18th birthday."[2] What does this tell you about the vital role parents can and should play in the formation of faith in their children?

78. Do you have any additional thoughts about why Paul would place this requirement in the list of qualifications for Elders?

79. What are your thoughts regarding a parent's intentional discipling of their children?

80. Do you think this means that your children have to be Christians? Would your answer depend at all on the child's age?

81. How do you feel about the idea that you have a duty to teach your children about the LORD?

82. Describe how your relationship with Christ impacts the way your children will view their own relationship with Christ.

Keeping his children submissive – Titus 1:6, 1 Timothy 3:4-5

Paul's logic in this requirement is powerful. To make sure we don't miss the impact of what he's trying to say, I've written out the passage from 1 Timothy 3:4-5.

He must manage his own household well, with all dignity keeping his children submissive, for if someone does not know how to manage his own household, how will he care for God's church?

Paul is clearly using the way a man leads and manages his household, and in particular his children's behavior, as a gauge for assessing the man's ability to oversee things in his role as an Elder. Follow the logic carefully... If a man's children are disobedient or insubordinate, they are demonstrating something about... their dad. They are showing that their dad does not possess the ability or wisdom to effectively oversee his own family in a godly manner. On the other hand, their godly and respectful obedience serves as an outward indication of the effectiveness and wisdom of their dad.

Paul's conclusion is stated in the form of a question. Here's my paraphrase: "How can a man expect to adequately oversee the leadership of God's church, made up of many adults from varying backgrounds, if he is unable to do so with his own children?" Many today balk at statements of this sort. They seem overly critical, judgmental, and harsh. But the severity of the statement Paul makes here is no weaker than the one Jesus Himself made in the parable of the talents when He said,

Well done, good and faithful servant. You have been faithful over a little; I will set

---

[2]Used by permission – the Barna Group - "Evangelism is Most Effective Among Kids" - October 11, 2004 - http://www.barna.org

THE EXTERNAL QUALIFICATIONS OF AN ELDER

*you over much. Enter into the joy of your master. - **Matthew 25:21, 23***

A person who shows themselves responsible and capable on a smaller scale is the type of person who can be trusted to be responsible and capable on a larger scale. This is true in the workplace. On athletic teams it's also true. And in the church, it is true as well. Paul's logic is right on the money.

This brings us to a difficult and sometimes controversial aspect of this topic. What about children who are older – teenagers and young adults who may be showing signs of rebellion or rejection of the faith? They are much more independent and responsible for their own choices than younger children, so do these criteria apply in those situations? Admittedly, this is a more difficult issue, but Paul provides some clear principles to guide us.

First, we must understand that a relationship with our children in their early years (especially ages 3 to 10) that includes consistent and loving discipline and heart-level teaching and application of God's word, will normally make this type of scenario much less likely. Children who observe a vital and genuinely personal faith in their parents and are actively drawn into that faith in those early years, seldom turn into rebellious teens. They learn to love Jesus for themselves, just as mom and dad love Jesus. He becomes more than a religious figure or Sunday school answer – He's a person to them, an intimate part of their lives that endures – even into the teen years.

Secondly, we must consider what it **means** if a man who is being considered for the role of Elder has a teen who is rebellious. Based on Paul's logic, it appears that a rebellious teen is a warning sign. What is it warning of? There may have been and possibly *still* may be some places of weakness in the man's life as a father and discipler of his own family. Like a pain in your body, a rebellious could be an outward indication of a more significant problem. These situations have to be considered very carefully and discussed with the man in question very frankly. It could be that instead of becoming an Elder the man has some urgent work to do at home.

As for a young adult, a different dynamic is involved. The child in question here is living in the adult world, making his or her own choices about life, lifestyle, and other important matters on a daily basis. The majority of times, as is wholly appropriate, these decisions are made without the input or "permission" of their parents. While still one of the man's children, they are much more than a child – they are an adult. They are responsible to God for themselves. They are responsible for their own choices, however far afield from the faith of their parents those choices may or may not be.

For that reason, I do not believe that a man being considered for Elder should automatically be disqualified because his adult children are living in ungodly ways. Adult children, raised in godly homes, are capable of their own adult disobedience to what they know and have been taught to be true. Look at your own life. How often, even in the past 6 months can you point to situations where you did something that *you* knew was not pleasing to God? The same is true of adult children. Their choices as adults are between them and the Lord and should not automatically be seen as a reflection on their parents.

However, there are instances where the behavior of a disobedient or rebellious young adult can be traced back to insufficient or inadequate parenting from earlier years. In this case, the troubling behavior seen during the young adult years is a symptom of parental struggles in earlier years. It's similar to lung cancer diagnosed today being indicative of a smoking habit many years earlier.

If this is the case, those close to the family or the parents themselves, may have knowledge of repeated struggles between parent and child in the formative or teen years that demonstrate a pattern of inadequate parenting in the past. If, after careful consideration, this is found to be the case, then a great deal of prayer and thought should be given to the possibility that the man being considered has a demonstrated history of not being able to manage his own family well and should not be an Elder in the church.

On the other hand, it should also be considered that the Lord may have grown the man through those struggles and has produced a new-found wisdom and strength that does qualify him for the role of Elder. Decisions regarding these issues are not easy, don't have any textbook answers, and therefore must be prayerfully and carefully made.

Q & A

83. In your own words, describe how Paul compares a man's ability to lead and disciple his family with his ability to care for the church.

84. Why is that such a big issue?

85. As a dad, do you feel that you are doing what is needed in order to disciple your family well?

Must manage his own household well – 1 Timothy 3: 4-5

The word used here for "household" or "family" is the Greek word "Oikos" – which can mean either "home," or by implication, "family." Paul's intention seems to be that the household in which the family resides, is adequately cared for and overseen by the man of the house. This doesn't mean he's the "king of the castle" or a dictator in miniature, but that he takes the Christ-like responsibility of servant-leadership. Clearly, this applies to the behavior and attitudes of his children, but there seems to be more implied in this statement.

The husband is held primarily responsible for the healthy arrangement and organization of the home. This doesn't mean that the husband is expected to decorate the house, do all the cooking, organize the spice rack, etc. What it means is that he is to oversee the healthy operation of the home, taking the initiative to ensure that the overall environment of the home and the relationships in it are healthy and godly. Some practical areas where this principle may apply are:

- the *finances* of the home are in order and above board
- the *home itself* is well-kept and clean
- the *family routine is organized* in such a way that it brings health and harmony
- the *family is led* actively in the way of Christ

Just from reading that short list of possible applications, it becomes obvious that the man of the house must enlist the help and cooperation of others within the household to see that those

THE EXTERNAL QUALIFICATIONS OF AN ELDER

things happen – which leads us to the heart of Paul's meaning. A man must learn to use his God-given leadership skills to achieve those ends for which God holds him responsible – first in his home, and then possibly within the church.

In order to help you see how practical this requirement is, let's take a few moments to look at each of the areas we've highlighted as possible areas where a man should "manage his household well." As we do remember, these are only *some* of the possible ways this principle could be applied...

The finances of the home are in order and above board

Financial decisions reveal a great deal about a person – and their priorities. An extreme case is the alcoholic or drug addict who never has money to feed his family. Why? Because his habit is more important to him, and his finances show it. If a man who serves as Elder can legitimately say that his financial dealings are in order; then it means that they are assuming their proper place in his life and in the life of the family. To him, money neither means too much (1 *Timothy 6:10*) nor too little (*Proverbs 13:11*). He understands that money is a means through which he and his family receive the blessing of God.

The man who serves as an Elder in Jesus' church is careful to avoid the lure of money and as a result does not engage in schemes or shady dealings to gain more. Scripture speaks very clearly on this issue in Ecclesiastes 5:10, Matthew 6:24, and Hebrews 13:5. Take the time to read through those passages now. In each of them the issue is that of motive and heart desire.

A man who serves as an Elder cannot be motivated by the accumulation of things. Jesus was very clear about this in Luke 12:14. Perhaps this is some of the motive behind much use of credit in our day. We are not content with what we have, so we finance what we want. An Elder must be careful that he incurs as little debt as possible as a clear testimony that his heart is free from the love of money.

Financial issues, as they relate to a man's household, will directly relate to the church he is to lead. If he is unable to gain mastery over his personal finances, he will have the tendency to make the same kinds of mistakes when it comes to financial decisions on behalf of the church. Said in the opposite way; the care and integrity with which a man manages his personal finances gives evidence that he can be trusted with the finances of the church family.

Why is this so important? Because the money with which the church is supported is given freely, in an attitude of faith, by hard-working, faithful people. It is given with God's work in mind and for His purposes. Elders need to be very careful and wise in the manner in which they manage, use, and allot the monies that are entrusted to them by the church family. There is no room for greed, self-interest, or personal gain.

It probably does not need to be said, but personal-financial integrity includes the obedient discipline of financial giving to the work of God. Obedience to God in financial giving is one of the many ways that Elders must set an example for the people they lead. An Elder who pretends to lead the church in a godly way but is not giving obediently out of his own finances is like a father who says, "Don't smoke..." to his children as he lights up his next cigarette. It is hypocrisy, plain and simple. Elders must be sure that they are good examples of faithful financial giving. But the issue of example in this area is more than simply being able to say, "Do what I do." It is a practical demonstration that you really care for the advancement and future of God's work in and through the church.

Q & A

86. Pretend for a moment that you are a person who is critical of the church. What are some ways you would look for problems within the church or its leaders that have to do with finances?

87. Based on your answer to that last question, why is it vital that church leaders are careful financially, both personally and as a church leadership team?

88. Do you have any ideas as to how Elders can put safeguards in place to make any accusations of a financial nature more easily refuted?

The home itself is well-kept and clean

One of the basic principles of life, seen in all areas – from natural phenomenon, to personal relationships, to individual behavior – is this: The outer reflects the inner. To better understand what I mean, think of these examples...

- Mealy apples indicate that the tree they come from is not healthy.
- Outbursts of anger from a wife toward her husband show that there are relational problems of some kind in their marriage.
- A disorganized, unkempt lifestyle reveals that there is something on a deeper level that is not in order.

Solomon said it this way,

Even a child makes himself known by his acts, by whether his conduct is pure and upright. - **Proverbs 20:11**

Do you see the connection Solomon makes between the inward life and the outer expression of it? He says that even a child's internal health can be evaluated by the type of actions that he produces outwardly. You can tell the general condition of the inner life by looking at what comes out of it, in the visible realm that can be seen. The clear implication is that if this is true for a child, it is also true of an adult – and even a family.

This applies not only to personal behavior toward other people, but also the actions that make up our daily life. If a person is lazy in their times with the Lord, we can tell that for some reason they do not desire fellowship with the Lord as they should. If a person does not organize their life in some way (schedule, lists, etc.), we can tell that their understanding of stewardship as it relates to the gift of time is lacking in some way. If a person's home is in a constant state of clutter and disorganization, we can see that there is some deeper issue at play that is resulting in the outer clutter. Jesus said it this way,

THE EXTERNAL QUALIFICATIONS OF AN ELDER

For no good tree bears bad fruit, nor again does a bad tree bear good fruit, for each tree is known by its own fruit. - **Luke 6:43**

    We often think of the fruit mentioned in this verse as evangelistic outreach or fruit in our character such as the fruit of the Spirit (Galatians 5). Those definitely qualify, but it seems more appropriate to understand that Jesus' words here simply mean the produce or outgrowth of a person's life. In that light, everything that flows out of our lives is fruit! Jesus wants the lives of His people to be constantly improving in every area! In this way the wealth of good fruit that flows out of us demonstrates His mighty ability to transform human beings into marvelous reflections of Him!

    If you are to become an Elder of Jesus' church, you must always go back to the issue of example (*1 Peter 5:3*). You need to look at the various areas of your life (attitudes, finances, home life, relationships, orderliness, and many more...) with this question in your mind, "Would I feel good about others within the church following my example in this area?" If not, you have some work to do.

    When it comes to orderliness in our homes, the task is not as simple as it may sound. While a man is responsible for the overall tone and direction of his home, including the orderliness of his household, his wife plays a very vital and key role in bringing it about. Paul instructs wives to be "*busy at home*" (*Titus 2:5*), which shows us that the care and organization of the home falls mainly within her realm of responsibility.

    So how does a man go about ensuring that he is following the scriptural command to "*manage his household well,*" given that his wife is the one who mainly oversees the cleanliness and order of the home? Is he to be a dictator, demanding that she keep house the way that he thinks best? Is he to micromanage every action she takes to determine if she is living up to the right standards of cleanliness and organization? Is he to take over those aspects of the home life altogether? If there is a problem in this area of orderliness in the home, none of these solutions addresses it, because all are clear violations of other scriptural principles.

    So, what is the answer? Once again, the issue for the man becomes one of leadership within the family. If there is a problem in this area, the beginning of a man's responsibility is to partner with his wife in seeking to understand God's heart on the matter. Only then can they effectively communicate God's heart to their children and apply it to their lives as a family. Let's take a moment to explore what is really on God's heart about this issue of household orderliness.

    In general, God's desire is for our lives to progressively display more of Him. As we grow in the Lord, those around us should see more and more evidence of His presence and touch in our lives. Naturally, this means that the various aspects of our character should be growing into His likeness, which should include the way we handle the responsibilities of life. In this way we demonstrate how He's filled our lives with a new and living hope, and those who see it have reason to wonder what has made such a dramatic change (*1 Peter 3:15*). One of the many areas in which we are to reflect His character by becoming more like Him is in the area of orderliness.

    The idea that our sense of orderliness reflects the orderly nature of God may be a bit foreign to you, so let's look at it. First off, the created universe shows God's creative and organizational abilities. He's the Master craftsman. Have you ever taken the time to carefully watch a true craftsman? There is purpose and meaning in everything they do. Every step of the creative process is done with meticulous care and concern. The creative process is carefully carried out, step by step, to ensure excellence in the final outcome.

We see the same thing in the way the created order functions. From the smallest microbe to the largest creature, each one is crafted with precision and care to function with amazing ability. Not only is each creature or organism crafted with care and intricacy, they also work together with clockwork precision to make the entirety of creation function in a mind-boggling way! That is testimony of how God works as the Master craftsman, with purpose, organization, and care.

Moving into the realm of the church, we find God likening believers to a human body, the perfect example of life-giving orderliness (*Ephesians 4*). As His body, we are to function in an orderly way, and toward that end He provides all kinds of organizational instructions. He teaches us regarding worship, the use of spiritual gifts, and even in relational issues between believers such as how we are to love one another (*1 Corinthians chapters 12-15*).

In each of these instances, His instructions center around the order with which things are to be done. Church leaders are to be chosen in a particular way, gifts are to be used according to particular guidelines, and church discipline is to be carried out in a certain pattern and progression. In all of these areas Paul says things are to be done "*decently and in order*" (*1 Corinthians 14:40*). Even our spiritual walk itself is to be implemented with a sense of order (*Colossians 2:5*).

How does all of this apply to us? God is a God of order – and being created in His image we have the honor and responsibility of portraying that aspect of His character through the way we live. The primary areas in which we do this are those that relate to our personal lives – our homes, our personal schedules, our daily routine. And as with everything God instructs, not only do we have the honor of reflecting something of Him, there is great benefit to us when we follow His example.

This is where the rubber meets the road in this area of keeping ones household in order. These are the elementary biblical concepts that a man and his wife must understand together and then discuss with their children. As the head of his home, the man is to take the lead in making sure that he and his wife are leading their children to understand the glorious opportunity and serious responsibility they have to bring glory to God by demonstrating His orderliness through their home. It's closely related to the parable of the stewards, with the man and his family being the stewards, and the home and the possessions that fill it being the talents. Their careful use and management of the Master's talents in a way that honors Him is an act that will enable them to hear, "*Well done, good and faithful servant*" (Matthew 25:23).

If a man does not take the lead in promoting and providing this kind of atmosphere for his family, unhealthy patterns and attitudes will grow. For instance, a household where finances are always short because of mounting debt or lack of a family budget will inevitably lead to arguments, insecurity, fear, and apprehension – not to mention the stress of persistent creditors and overdue bills. When a man allows his home to be cluttered or dirty many negative things will arise. Frustration, feelings of hopelessness, stress, and the increased likelihood of sickness are some possible outcomes. But even more damaging is the bad example he and his wife are setting for their children (which they could very well imitate when they are adults).

But the impact stretches outside the walls of his home too. People are less likely to want to visit due to the increased amount of clutter or uncleanliness in their home. His children may feel embarrassed to invite friends over due to their living conditions. Practically, the family is less able to be hospitable. As a natural consequence, they reduce their potential for ministry to those in their church and community. Those outside their family who know their situation will begin to lose respect for them as Christians, somehow knowing instinctively that such conditions should not exist where Christ is Lord. In short, a lack of leadership in this area can have far-reaching repercussions.

We can easily connect this idea with Paul's qualifications for Elders and the connection he makes between a man's ability to manage his home and his ability to manage the church. What would come of a church that was not adequately organized? What would be the result if those within the church were not guided in the biblical instructions for worship, use of spiritual gifts, church conflict or church discipline? How could a church function rightly if those entrusted with its leadership did not do their job of caring for, organizing, and leading the body into right relationship with God and each other? How could the church facilities feel hospitable to outsiders if they were sloppily cared for, cluttered, or generally disorganized? And what if the leadership did not see the need to address such things or to teach the people of the church that such habits of neglect reflect badly on God? What would become of such a church? What impact would it have on its neighbors? The point Paul is making seems very clear – an effective church leader will only be so when he is an effective leader at home first.

As in every area, these general concepts can be taken to extremes, and we should be careful not to make that mistake. Perfectionism is not the answer. Each of us must develop a healthy, balanced reflection of the orderly nature of God. An obsession with cleanliness or orderliness will demonstrate an inner problem just as much as a complete disregard for them would. These are areas where we need to show responsibility and diligence in the stewardship of our lives and possessions and do so in a manner that honors God. For a man considering the role of Elder, this area should be well in hand in his private life before he is ready to lead the church.

Q & A

89. Some important areas of household oversight have been mentioned above (finances, etc.). What other areas of household management can you think of that could be taken into account?

90. Write your thoughts on the responsibility of leaders in the church to progressively reflect God's character by the way they live.

91. Explain how you see orderliness in life reflecting God's character?

92. Are there any steps you feel you should take to improve in this area of managing your household well?

The family routine is organized

It's not unusual in our day for families to be moving at the speed of sound from the moment they rise until their heads hit the pillow exhausted at night. Weekends are crammed full of activities for parents and children, often at multiple places at the same time! Yet, few seem to stop and consider whether it is healthy for their family to be living at such a hectic pace. As the head of our homes, we are responsible to ensure that our families are learning wisdom in regards to the activities and events that they are involving themselves in. Being too busy is *not* a healthy or godly thing.

biblically, we can draw some great help from the principles taught in God's "sabbath" command (*Exodus 20:8-11*). Though it is clear from the New Testament that the sabbath command is not one that Christians are to legalistically observe (*Colossians 2:16*), there is nevertheless a great benefit to implementing its principles into our lives. In the past, the church has promoted the idea that the sabbath is to be a day of family worship. But there is only one context where the sabbath is spoken of where that idea is even hinted at (*Leviticus 23:3*). The other passages that speak of the sabbath refer to it as a day for God's people to rest.

When God speaks of remembering the sabbath to keep it holy, He means that the sabbath is to be faithfully and *purely* observed, as it was meant to be observed... and that is as a day of rest. It is in these times of rest that we can recuperate from our busy lives and prepare for what may lie ahead. It is during these times that we find refreshment, encouragement, and are able to hear the often quiet voice of the Lord leading us in the direction we need to go. How important it is that we are leading our families into this vitally important discipline of a balanced family routine that provides the rest and the activity that God intends!

This idea is completely foreign to our modern mindset. It wouldn't surprise me if the idea takes you a bit off guard right now. For some reason we've come to believe that we don't have enough time to do what we need to do, much less be able to take an entire day off for rest! Even thinking of taking a day to rest gives us feelings of wasting time rather than wise stewardship of it. The truth is that such thinking is from the world, not from God. God's way is the best way – and that way includes a regularity to our intentional times of rest.

As our Creator, God knows that we cannot go full-tilt for very long without losing our ability to live in a healthy way. In fact, God prescribed a full day of rest for His people every 7th day to ensure that they were remaining physically, emotionally, and spiritually healthy. And He took this instruction so seriously that He often brought judgment on those who ignored or disregarded the sabbath.

What lessons should we glean from these ideas? Obviously, the commitment to a regular time of rest, for us and for our families, should be a major priority for us. It's not only what God Himself prescribed for His people in the Old Testament, but also what goes along with the way we are wired. Just as your car needs regular oil changes and maintenance, your spirit needs a time to rest, refresh, and prepare for the future. The sabbath day of rest is just what the owner's manual has instructed.

When we fail to make regular rest a priority for us and our families many negative things begin to happen. Stress creeps in and anxiety levels rise. Not only do schedules begin to conflict, but anger and resentment often come along with those conflicts. Our children grow up learning to rush from here to there with no down time. They begin to feel that they must say "yes" to every good opportunity instead of wisely choosing which activities and groups are best for them. It is our responsibility, as the head of our homes, to ensure that our families are operating according to what is healthy and godly in the organization of their schedules.

How we practically do this varies with the individual and his family. Some strictly adhere to Sunday being their "sabbath" since everyone is off work or school anyway. Others, like many who are in full-time ministry choose another day of the week as their "day off." The idea is that you need to find some way to ensure that you and your family are being intentional about scheduling in regular and consistent times of rest, so that you are able to make the most of the lives the Lord God has given you, for His glory!

Q & A

93. What frustrations have you felt in the past due to busy and conflicting schedules within your own family?

94. From your experience, what does ongoing stress of this nature do to the family as a whole?

95. Explain what you understand as the purpose of a "sabbath?"

96. Do you have places in your schedule when you and your family plan "down time?"

97. What steps do you need to take to provide a better opportunity for rest in your family's routine?

The family is led actively in the way of Christ

Much has already been said about the role each Elder needs to play in the spiritual growth and discipleship of his own family. The only remaining point is to stress that this responsibility needs to be intentional, and one that each man finds his best way to accomplish. Some will utilize a regular family worship time, while another may work individually with each member of his family. No matter the method, each man needs to make sure that his family is learning to love God more, and honor, understand, and apply the scriptures to their lives. Regular church attendance, personal times in the scriptures, and an ongoing lifestyle of prayer are things he should be teaching, modeling, and encouraging in the members of his family.

These are just some of the possible areas that an Elder should be aware of "managing his household well." Now let's move back to some other external qualifications...

Is not a recent convert – 1 Timothy 3:6

Nobody would ask a first year physics student to take on the oversight of the entire physics department at a major scientific development firm. No one would expect a 12 year old computer whiz to take over product development for Microsoft. But it is often the case that people who are relatively new to the faith are asked to take on a leadership role within the church. One of the main reasons this happens is that clear evidence of spiritual growth is exciting to see. We get encouraged when we see someone relatively new to the faith growing, grasping more scriptural truth, and having their lives transformed. In the bright light of the exciting and positive spiritual developments in their lives, we fail to remember that a good deal of maturity comes in the time-tested trenches of endurance.

Paul's instruction is a very apt reminder that we are to be careful that our excitement about new fruit doesn't overcome our wisdom and spiritual discernment. But Paul's caution in this area has another aspect to it. His concern is not only for the church, but also for the man being considered. Paul says that if a man is allowed to serve as an Elder before he is ready, then *"he may become conceited and fall under the same judgment as the devil."* (*1 Timothy 3:5*) This is a very serious concern that we would do well to consider for a moment.

The dictionary defines "conceit" as, "an excessively favorable opinion of one's own ability or importance." Imagine the scenario Paul is describing... a man has genuinely placed his faith in Christ and out of genuine love for God has begun to grow rapidly in the new-found joy of his faith. He's finding great peace, contentment, and satisfaction in the truths of God's word as they are revealed to him. His excitement is contagious, and many within his church family are encouraged and excited just being around him. It's not long before those who lead the church are taking note of the wonderful things Christ is doing in his life. They ask him to consider becoming a co-leader of God's work with them. What happens within the man when this kind of opportunity is presented to him?

Paul says that a situation like this is fertile soil for a very negative attitude – conceit. The man can easily slip into believing that he is uncommon, that he's grown so quickly because there is something special about him. He starts to think that the same qualities that brought such rapid growth will also enable him to serve as an uncommonly good leader for the church. His focus has subtly shifted from Christ's work in him to his own ability.

Don't think for a moment that the scenario I've just painted is far-fetched. It happens repeatedly in the life of the church. The lures of sin are subtle, never announcing themselves in broad daylight. But when they strike, they go deep – to the core of who we are as individuals, corrupting God's good work in us by pointing us to faith in ourselves rather than continued child-like faith in Christ alone.

As Paul says, this is the same route that the devil took when his plunge into Godless rebellion began. When we, like him, allow conceit to become active in our souls, we will experience the judgment of God as he does. Paul's instruction here is not only to save the church the heartache and pain that comes from conceited, self-aggrandizing leadership, but also to save the new convert from the trap of conceit that awaits him when he rushes too soon into a position of leadership.

This raises the question, "How new is too new?" Paul wisely does not answer that question. I say it's wise because the answer will be different for each person. Some churches do create time-based guidelines to make the decision a bit clearer for them... 2 years as a believer, 5 years actively involved in the church, etc. While these may prove to be good cautionary guidelines, they still fail to address the heart of the issue.

Each man who comes into the role of Elder leadership needs to have had enough experience in his faith that he can demonstrate a track record of consistency, dependability, and wise action. Honestly, he needs to have weathered some storms in his life and come out with his faith stronger as a result. There needs to be some experience with the real, everyday struggles of life and the constant battle it is to cling to and apply faith in them. A man who is ready to lead the church is one who is well versed in the scriptures and the wise application of them to the most difficult of situations. He needs to be seasoned, mature, and ready for the heavy burden of church leadership.

Jesus came to live and die for the sake of His church. It is the most important and powerful group of people on the planet. Doesn't the church deserve the best leadership we can give it? Intuitively that has to mean that we don't put people into the role of Elder who are not ready for it. It would not be fair to any man who was placed in that position, but even more seriously, it would not be right for the church.

That is one reason that this Elder Training Handbook has been designed as it has. The areas you are covering in this training are what I consider "must know" information for those who desire to lead the church of Jesus Christ. In honestly and diligently completing this coursework you are putting yourself into a place of readiness to lead God's church with skill, wisdom, and faith. Stay with it, God has great things ahead!

Q & A

98. Describe a problem you could see a new convert having, if he was placed into Elder leadership too quickly. What result would this have on the church they are leading?

99. In evaluating your own spiritual walk, where do you see yourself – on the end of the "new convert" or toward the "mature" side? Be careful how you make your evaluation... time doesn't automatically translate into maturity!

Must be well thought of by outsiders – 1 Timothy 3:7

Does this requirement seem strange to you? Why do church leaders need to be of good reputation in circles *outside* the church? Paul says that it is so that the individual leader "*may not fall into disgrace, into a snare of the devil.*" The stories of this kind of disgrace are numerous. Typically, it involves a Pastor, but periodically you hear of a lay-leader who is involved in some sort of scandal as well. Embezzlement, abuse, improper sexual relationships, pornography addictions. These are the lines that blaze across the newscasts when a Christian leader sins. It's a disgrace to the individual, but also to the church he has served. Those outside the church find ammunition for their attacks, ridicule, and disdain of the church – and Jesus is dishonored.

Disgrace of this kind harms the work of Christ. The leaders of His church must be continually aware of this possibility and carefully ensure that there is no room for outsiders to accuse them and thereby bring disgrace on the church. A situation I recently heard about illustrates the importance of this concept powerfully.

A woman had been a faithful member of her church for many years. During that time, she had served as a Deacon, been the leader of the Children's Ministry, youth choir, and many other very popular and successful ministry programs within the church. There were many people in the church who appreciated her faithful and professional service to the children and families and were very supportive of her personally. But another life was being lived outside the walls of the church.

Those outside the church knew her as a critical, dissatisfied person. They experienced her contentious and difficult spirit, and from her lips they heard expression of beliefs that were in direct contradiction to what the scriptures taught about Jesus. But they also knew she was a Deacon at her church.

What do you think those outsiders thought about her? More importantly, what do you think they thought about a church that would allow her to be in such a prominent place of leadership? The situation brought disgrace on the church and on her, eventually destroying the church – all because the leaders of the church were not careful to follow the scriptural principles for choosing leaders.

At this point it is good for us to recognize that no person who is faithfully serving as a leader in the local church will have 100% positive reviews from those outside the church. The faithful life of a Christian will often be received badly, bringing about a negative reaction. They may say the person is "holier-than-thou", a "preacher man", or some other derogatory term. They may even trump up false accusations about the person so that his reputation is tarnished in the eyes of the community. But what is important to keep in mind is that while such accusations will be made from time to time, they should have absolutely *no* basis of truth to them. The Christian leader must be careful that his life is being lived "above reproach" so that no accusations have foundation.

Q & A

100. What impact do you think an "outsider's" negative opinion of a man who is a church Elder has on (a) the man? (b) his church? (c) the Lord?

101. How do you think a situation should be handled if a man who is already a church Elder is accused of bad conduct outside the church, but there is no obvious evidence?

102. How do you think a situation should be handled where a man who is already a church Elder is found to have a legitimately bad reputation with those outside the church?

WRITTEN QUIZ

In the following questions, do your best to answer without reviewing this section. If you have trouble recalling the information, don't worry – you'll discuss your answers with your mentor!

- What does Paul mean when he says that an Elder must be "*the husband of one wife?*"

- What are some of the areas in a man's personal life and behavior where this standard should be applied?

- Explain why this issue is of such great importance when considering possible church

THE EXTERNAL QUALIFICATIONS OF AN ELDER

leaders?

- What does Paul mean when he says that an Elder's children must be "*faithful?*"

- Why is this an important gauge of a man's ability to lead the church?

- What does Paul mean when he says that an Elder's children must be "*obedient?*" How is this different from "*faithful?*"

- Why is this an important gauge of a man's ability to lead the church?

- What does Paul mean when he says that an Elder must "*manage his own household well?*"

- What are some of the practical areas where this principle should be applied?

- How is that an important barometer of the man's potential as an Elder?

- Why should church leaders be careful to ensure that only mature, proven believers are added to the church's leadership?

- Explain why an Elder candidate should be evaluated in light of the opinions of those outside the church.

SELF EVALUATION EXERCISE

In light of the qualifications, we've explored in this section, evaluate yourself in each of the categories listed in the section below. You will rate yourself in each category on a 1 to 10 scale regarding where you are at this point. Be careful to be honest with yourself, assessing where you are now, not where you'd like to be. Underneath each you will have the opportunity to include what you are doing to grow or improve in each particular area if you would like to include that information.

An Elder must...

    be the husband of one wife,
        <u>Rating & Comments:</u>

    have children who are faithful
        <u>Rating & Comments:</u>

have children who are obedient
    Rating & Comments:

manage his own household well
    Rating & Comments:

not be a new convert
    Rating & Comments:

have a good reputation with those outside the church
    Rating & Comments:

SCRIPTURE MEMORIZATTON
Even a child makes himself known by his acts, by whether his conduct is pure and upright.
Proverbs 20:11

SECTION 4

The Internal Qualifications Of An Elder

As with any position, only certain types of individuals are fit to serve in the position of Elder. This doesn't mean that every Elder must like the same things or have similar personalities. It means that every man who becomes an Elder must have specific spiritual characteristics and personal abilities that equip him to adequately serve the church in the demanding role of Elder. In this section, we will examine the remaining biblical qualifications for the role of Elder.

Specifically, this section will be addressing the qualifications in Paul's lists that we might refer to as character or spiritual qualifications. These qualifications are referring more to **who** you are as a person than **what** you are able to do. For example, a person who is very capable on a business or professional level but is also sexually immoral is automatically and quite quickly removed from consideration for the role of Elder because his character is not up to the standard required. You may be able to be "successful" in other roles while still having a tainted character, but it is impossible to be qualified for the role of Elder if that is true of you.

What matters most for Elders is that they are spiritually mature, growing not only in their knowledge of the Savior, but also in their inner strength and faith in Him. Paul gives quite an exhaustive list of such qualities in his letters to Timothy and Titus, two young church leaders who were told to appoint Elders for the leadership of their local churches. The requirements Paul gives serve as a checklist of sorts, to ensure that we are able to clearly identify those who are ready and able to serve as Elders. In this section we'll be looking at each of these in more detail.

As we do so, be aware that our format is changing a bit at this point. Throughout this section you will be given a much shorter, to the point definition of each characteristic. Then you will be asked to respond to some made-up scenarios. The goal of the scenario exercises is not to trick you, but to help you think through some situations you may very well face as an Elder someday, in light of the scriptural characteristics that are to be true of Elders. Try not to think whether the situation would really be able to happen in your life, just imagine what you would do if it did.

Above reproach – 1 Timothy 3:2 / Titus 1:7

This does not mean that an Elder needs to be perfect. But he does need to be a man whose life shows a high regard for God's holy instructions about life and is *consistent* in living according to them. There should be no areas of his life where he is legitimately worthy of blame. Take some time to consider each situation below and write out how you think the Elder who is "*above reproach*" should respond.

- He is given $10 too much change when checking out at the store, and he doesn't notice it until he gets home.

- A scandal at his work appears to implicate him in misconduct, but he is really innocent.

- His adolescent son is caught cheating on a final exam.

- While having a quiet coffee at his favorite spot, he sees a young lady in her early twenties who his family knows well. She is crying and asks if she can talk to him someplace private.

- He is asked to help collect the morning financial offering at church. When he is finished, he realizes that the other man who helped collect the offering has left him alone with the money that was collected.

- One of his superiors at work is genuinely mistreating him and he doesn't know why.

Disciplined – Titus 1:8

A person who is disciplined is one who is not known to be a person of extremes. He is well-balanced and moderate in his perceptions, opinions, and actions. Take some time to consider each situation below and write out how you think the Elder who is "*disciplined*" should respond.

- His teenage daughter was taking her best friend to the mall and received two traffic tickets – one for speeding and another for reckless driving.

- He has been working on a real estate investment deal for 6 months and finds out that the bank is pulling his financing, shutting down the possibility of going through with the deal.

- A man in the church is being "pushy" toward him about a decision the Elders have been praying about. It's clear the man will not be happy unless things go as he would like.

- His wife is very upset with him about something he said to her the night before. She is accusing him of neglecting her, though he feels he's been very nurturing lately. Her comments are making him very angry.

- Someone who holds a political viewpoint that is opposite to the Elder's is trying to engage him in debate about current political issues. As the Elder is hearing the first

THE INTERNAL QUALIFICATIONS OF AN ELDER

comments from the person, his passion about his viewpoint is beginning to rise.

- A man in the church appears to be very hypocritical in his lifestyle – living a "loose" morality, while at the same time being verbally condemning toward others . The Elder is asked to talk to the man about his attitude.

Self-controlled – 1 Timothy 3:2 / Titus 1:8

A person who is self-controlled is careful to do what is right in God's sight in all circumstances and is typically successful in doing so. Take some time to consider each situation below and write out how you think the Elder who is "*self-controlled*" should respond.

- The Elder has a life-long hobby collecting something of interest to him (you fill in the blank for yourself – guns, stamps, baseball cards, audio equipment). He's always wanted a certain item for his collection and finds it at a bargain price. The previous evening, he and his wife had discussed how they need to trim their spending in order to stay within their budget.

- At an office party the Elder discovers that the dessert being served is the most delicious he's ever tasted. He's already had two servings and is offered a third... it's REALLY good!

- At a church event the Elder is involved in a fun conversation with a group of men. One of them makes an off-color comment that is truly funny, and which causes the entire group to laugh. A clever, equally off-color response pops into the Elder's head.

- A small but influential group of people who attend his church have begun to promote something called "open theology." While at home, watching his favorite television program, he receives a distressed call from a small group leader asking him to come to his small group the next evening, where some of those people attend, to discuss the issue with some members of the group who are very confused. He has to work all day the next day.

Respectable – 1 Timothy 3:2

A person who is known to be respectable is one whose conduct and character cause others to think highly of him, even when he may not have been treated well himself. Take some time to consider each situation below and write out how you think the Elder who is "*respectable*" should respond.

- The Elder walks into a classroom at the church to find a group of 10 year old boys with tables turned sideways on the floor, throwing Bibles across the room at each other.

- While driving home on the interstate, he is cut off *and* flipped-off by a 20-something young man. He almost runs off the road trying to avoid the car as it has suddenly swerved in front of him.

- While eating at his favorite restaurant with his family, the waiter spills a drink down the front of his wife's blouse. He has the feeling it might have been done on purpose.

- A group of people at church are discussing whether to help a person in the church family who is known to have a drinking problem and has lost his job as a result. Few people think the man deserves help – most just mention what a "bum" he is.

- A doctrinal dispute has broken out in the church. An all-church meeting has been called to hear the positions and discuss the matter. One man, clearly in the wrong doctrinally speaking, is very hostile toward anyone who doesn't agree with his position. The man challenges the Elder directly during the meeting.

Hospitable – 1 Timothy 3:2 / Titus 1:8

A person who is hospitable is one who is warm and receptive toward strangers or guests. Take some time to consider each situation below and write out how you think the Elder who is *"hospitable"* should respond.

- A stranger comes into the church on a Sunday morning after the service has begun. The Elder notices that he is quiet, very reserved, and doesn't look at anyone. During the greeting time, he notices that when others approach the man and speak to him, he is very short and fairly unresponsive. Those who greet him just look confused and turn away.

- After a hard day at work and a noisy dinner, the Elder is about to sit down to a movie with his family when the doorbell rings. At the door is a family from the church who was in the neighborhood and decided to drop in.

- The Elder is walking down the street and sees a man sitting on the curb who is dirty, unkempt, and clearly living on the street. As he approaches, the man asks him if he can spare some change.

- Thanksgiving is coming up, and the Elder becomes aware of a college student in the church who will be remaining in town due to financial inability to return home.

- The Elder is busy at his desk, completing some long-overdue bill-paying when his son comes in and asks him a question about "Spider Man".

THE INTERNAL QUALIFICATIONS OF AN ELDER

Not a drunkard – 1 Timothy 3:3

The meaning of this one is fairly obvious, though sometimes misunderstood. This means that the Elder is not one who is prone to being drunk or under the influence of any substance. It does not mean that an Elder cannot have an alcoholic drink (remember that the common drink of the day in Paul's time was a watery sort of wine), but that he is not to be drunk. Take some time to consider each situation below and write out how you think the Elder who is *"not a drunkard"* should respond.

- The Elder and his family are invited to the home of a new attender of the church for a Super Bowl party. At the party, the host offers the Elder a beer to drink and he accepts. Later in the day, the host's wife offers him another.

- In the years before the Elder came to Christ, alcohol abuse was a problem for him. Since becoming a Christian, he has learned from scripture that drinking in moderation is not wrong. He still likes the taste of alcohol and would like to keep a 6 pack or bottle of wine in his house. What should he do, and why?

Not violent but gentle – 1 Timothy 3:3

A man who is gentle is not a push-over but *is* known to be careful and kind in how he deals with people. Notice the contrast in this verse... he's *not* to be violent, *but* gentle. He understands that people are valuable and many times fragile. He knows that the anger of man does not accomplish the purposes of God (*James 1:20*). Take time to consider each situation below and write out how you think the Elder who is "gentle" should respond.

- A woman in the church is known to be very combative. One morning at church, as people are milling about, the Elder is verbally accosted by the woman over a recent decision of the Elder Team.

- A co-worker at his job comes to the Elder, angrily accusing him of causing her to miss a deadline. In reality, he did the work he was assigned and passed it on to another person before she was to receive it.

Not quarrelsome – 1 Timothy 3:3

A person who is not quarrelsome is one who doesn't pick fights and isn't looking for fights. He is not argumentative, and he is not contentious. Take some time to consider each situation below and write out how you think the Elder who is *"not quarrelsome"* should respond.

- One man in the church is very passionate about issues surrounding the end times. He is convinced that his position is *the* biblical position and often speaks to people about it. During a small group discussion, the man begins prodding the Elder with questions about his beliefs regarding the end times. It soon becomes clear that the man is not satisfied with the Elder's responses, and he begins trying to paint the Elder's responses in such a way that the Elder appears to be unbiblical in his beliefs.

- The Elder's neighbor is guilty of repeatedly allowing his dog to cross the property line and poop in the Elder's yard. The Elder has spoken to him about it once before, but the dog still does his "doo-ty" on the Elder's lawn. It's becoming very annoying and is beginning to ruin the Elder's lawn.

Not a lover of money/not greedy for gain – 1 Timothy 3:3 / Titus 1:7

A person who is not a lover of money is one who uses money responsibly and sees it as a blessing from God. But they are also equally content with large or small amounts of money in their possession. They are careful to ensure that money does not control them. Someone who is not greedy for gain is a person who does not let greed or self-interest control them. Take some time to consider each situation below and write out how you think the Elder who is *"not a lover of money / not greedy for gain"* should respond.

- The Elder's brother introduces him to a business deal that is "guaranteed" to pay off big. The implications of the business presentation are that the Elder could possibly pay off all his debt and amass a significant savings within a few short years if he follows the program details step by step. It would require a commitment of $300 up front, and 20 hours a week for the first year.

- While doing his taxes, the Elder discovers that had he earned $100 less over the past year, he would have qualified for a one-time credit worth $1300 per child. His tax accountant tells him that since it is only a $100 difference, he might as well claim the credit – and receive $3900 for his 3 children.

A lover of good – Titus 1:8

A man who is a lover of good is one who is in touch with the heart of God in regard to what is good and right – and what is bad and sinful. He is careful to examine what he hears, sees, experiences, and says to ensure that everything in his life is in fact, good. Take some time to consider each situation below and write out how you think the Elder who is *"a lover of good"* should respond.

- The Elder is invited to go to a movie that is rated "R." He's seen many movies that carry that rating, mostly for war-type violence – so the rating alone is not his main concern. What sort of things should the Elder be considering in deciding if the movie outing is one he should attend as a *"lover of good?"*

- A very open disagreement has arisen in the church between two ladies. Each one has become deeply hurt and they are refusing to talk to one another. Their conflict is not causing obvious problems within the church, but the tension between them is very obvious.

- A few new families from a church across town that has split have been attending the Elder's church recently. They are all quite enjoyable to be with and appear to be demonstrating the fruit of the Spirit regularly. One of the families is very supportive of "word of faith" theology which claims that God wants his people to be rich, happy, and blessed. One Sunday morning the Elder overhears the father in one of these families speaking excitedly to others in the church about these beliefs.

Upright – Titus 1:8

For a man to be upright means that his life is generally free from compromise or impure motives. His personal and family standards are clearly in growing conformity with God's word and are consistent in their application. Take some time to consider each situation below and write out how you think the Elder who is *"upright"* should respond.

- The Elder's son is wanting to go to a concert with some friends. Upon further investigation the Elder discovers that the group is a ghetto rap trio that advocates violence against police. The Elder is disappointed, thinking that his son should have been more aware of how this type of entertainment does not honor God. What should he do?

- The Elder has gone to a movie with some people from the church. The reviews he's read, and the comments others have made about the move made it sound fairly wholesome. About a fourth of the way into the movie, a very sensual sex scene flashes onto the screen. Hoping that it will be brief, the Elder tries to wait it out, but it seems to drag on and on.

- The Elder is at the church office on Sunday morning and has been speaking with two young women who are having a personal conflict. Their conversation has been very beneficial and the two are reconciling tearfully. As they are preparing to leave, each one gives the Elder a hug. Just as he is beginning to hug one of them the other leaves the room as the church busy-body walks in to see them hugging.

- The Elder has gone to a town about 120 miles away to purchase supplies for the church using the church debit card. Taking longer than he expected, lunch came and went, and he has become very hungry. He goes to a fast-food place, places his order, and reaches for his wallet and discovers he has left it at home. The church debit card is the only "money" he has.

The following qualifications have been set apart in a separate section because they are less about who a man is, and more about what he is able to do. We have to face facts, some men are simply not able to do certain things that others are quite capable of doing. I cannot play basketball very well, but I can play the drums. I cannot do math worth anything, but I can teach. When it comes to the role of Elder there are certain abilities or capabilities that he must have. For this section, we'll revert to the previous format to flesh out what each area means.

Aspires to the office of Overseer – 1 Timothy 3:1

1 Timothy 3:1 says, *"The saying is trustworthy: If anyone aspires to the office of overseer, he desires a noble task."* In order for a man to serve as an Elder, the must be some kind of personal desire to serve in the position. But we must be careful...all of us are prone to wrong motives, and the same can be true when desiring to be an Elder. For some it may be a desire to be in a position of influence or power. For others, it could be a desire to be an Elder so that others will think well of them. There are likely many reasons a person might desire to be an Elder that are not wholly pure.

So, if Paul wants a man to *"desire"* to be an Elder, what might be some **good** reasons a man wants to fill the role? Perhaps he wants to pass along the blessing and knowledge that God has given to him; or he may have a heart of compassion for people and desires to lead them in right paths that honor God. For me, I ***long*** to be a leader of God's people because I want to do what I can, with the Lord's guidance and power, to enable the church to be healthy and strong, fulfilling God's purpose in the world.

Q & A

103. As you think about your desire to be an Elder, what are some of the questions you've asked about your motives?

104. What good motives do you see in your desires to be an Elder?

Able to teach – 1 Timothy 3:2

Given the Elder's role as doctrinal guardian of the flock, it only makes sense that a man who serves as an Elder must be capable of leading others in understanding and applying the teachings entrusted to us in the scriptures. Whether in a large group setting, or one on one, each man who serves on the Elder team must have the ability to lead others in better knowing and applying God's word.

Some read this requirement and become fearful, believing that they are not an "up front" kind of teacher like most Pastors, and therefore that they are not qualified to be an Elder. The truth is that teaching takes place on many different levels and the large group setting is only one of those. A man who is terrible at public speaking may be fabulous at leading one or two others in study and discussion of the scriptures. In that way, he is showing himself *"able to teach."*

Q & A

105. Would you consider yourself "able to teach?" On a scale of 1 to 10 where would you

rank yourself on being "able to teach?" (1 = not very capable and 10 = very capable)

106. Is the thought of teaching in a large group setting something that intimidates you? What about a small group or one on one situation?

107. Can you give an example or two where you have taught others (not necessarily in spiritual matters)?

Holds firmly to the trustworthy word as taught – Titus 1:9

The point Paul is making here is that an Elder needs to be grounded in his own faith in Christ to such an extent that he is not swayed from it. He knows what he believes, and **why** he believes it. Without this type of stability that flows from deep conviction, an Elder will be just as prone to unsteadiness in his faith as a young believer. That's not a very good quality to have in a leader of the church! Some of the sections in the later parts of this curriculum are designed to help you become stronger in these kinds of things. You need to be thoroughly equipped for the good work of being an Elder and those sections will help in that regard.

Q & A

108. What would you say the "*trustworthy*" word is that Paul is talking about in this verse?

109. Explain what would happen if an Elder was not able to hold firmly to these things.

110. Are there any areas in your knowledge or belief that you feel need to be strengthened, or areas where you need to increase your convictions? If so, what areas are those?

Able to give instruction in sound doctrine – Titus 1:9

Sound doctrine is at the core of the church. A wrong belief about a fundamental area can make the difference between a true believer and someone who is not. Elders must have a very firm grasp on sound doctrine, knowing the difference between spiritual truth and lies, as they hear them. But they have to be able to take it a step further and instruct others in those doctrines. An Elder needs to be able to hear the conflicts and struggles of a person's life and know what scriptures and biblical principles can apply to their situation in helpful ways. This is shepherding the church, guiding people to right thinking and right living in light of the scriptures.

Q & A

111. Based on *Philippians 2:1-7*, how would you counsel a couple who is squabbling over minor things in their relationship?

112. Are there any specific areas of doctrine that you feel you should know better? What are they?

Able to rebuke those who contradict sound doctrine – Titus 1:9

An obvious and important extension of the need to know and understand sound doctrine is the ability to recognize and refute bad doctrine. An Elder, and the team of Elders as a whole, must know their doctrine well so that they are able to do this as needed. Sadly, the average Christian doesn't normally take the time to read and understand the scriptures as they should, and as a result they may be easy victims of those who teach wrong or misleading doctrines.

Elders not only need to understand what doctrines are bad or wrong, they need to know *why* they are bad or wrong. Most times, the difference between right doctrine and wrong doctrine is in the twisting or misunderstanding of a few words. An Elder must be able to examine the variety of teachings that come to the forefront and compare them to the plain meaning of scripture so that they are able to make solid judgments in regard to their truthfulness. He must be able to see where the wrong beliefs lead in the end. This takes diligence, time, and a commitment to spiritual and intellectual growth on the part of every Elder. His passion for the truth of God along with his concern for the people of God should be instrumental in motivating him to understand and confront wrong doctrines as they arise.

Q & A

113. As an example, explain why it is wrong and harmful to believe that our "good works" can bring us into God's favor or earn His forgiveness.

114. Why do you think it is important for anyone (not only Elders) to be able to see the difference between good and bad doctrine? What is at stake?

115. On a 1 to 10 scale (1 being "poor" and 10 being "excellent"), how would you rate yourself in terms of your **desire** to be able to refute wrong doctrine?

116. On that same 1 to 10 scale, how would you rate yourself in terms of **ability** to refute bad doctrine?

117. What steps do you think are most important for you to take in order to improve in these areas?

The remainder of this curriculum is designed to guide you through a variety of topics you need to know in order to serve effectively as a shepherd of God's people. My desire is that you will apply yourself diligently to learning and growing in the areas covered so that you can be the kind of leader Jesus' church deserves.

THE INTERNAL QUALIFICATIONS OF AN ELDER

WRITTEN QUIZ

In the following questions, do your best to answer without reviewing this section. If you have trouble recalling the information, don't worry – you'll discuss your answers with your mentor!

- What does Paul mean when he says that an Elder must be "*above reproach?*"

- Define what it means for a man to be "*disciplined.*"

- What does Paul mean when he says that an Elder must be "*self-controlled?*"

- In what ways should an Elder be "*respectable?*"

- Explain how you understand Paul's teaching that an Elder should be "*hospitable?*"
- Define what it means to "*not be a drunkard.*"

- Are there any precautions an Elder *should* take regarding alcohol?

- What does Paul mean when he says that an Elder must be "*gentle?*"

- If a man is "*not quarrelsome,*" what kind of outward behaviors would you expect to see when he is in a combative situation?

- What is the difference between being a "*lover of money*" and being one who invests his money wisely and effectively?

- In your own words, describe what it means for an Elder to be a "*lover of good.*"

- Paul says that an Elder should be "*upright.*" What does that really mean?

- List some of the scenarios where you might be able to see if a man is "*able to teach.*"

- What is the "*trustworthy word*" that Paul says an Elder must "*hold firmly to?*"

- Paul says an Elder must be able to "*instruct in sound doctrine.*" Explain how you see this looking if he is not the teaching Pastor.

- What is needed by an Elder if he is to "*rebuke*" those who propose wrong doctrine?

SELF EVALUATION EXERCISE

In light of the qualifications, we've explored in this section, evaluate yourself in each of the categories listed. Underneath each you will have the opportunity to include what you are doing to grow or improve in each particular area if you would like to include that information.

An Elder must be...

    above reproach

    Comments:

    disciplined

    Comments:

    self-controlled

    Comments:

    respectable

    Comments:

THE INTERNAL QUALIFICATIONS OF AN ELDER

hospitable

Comments:

a man who is not a drunkard

Comments:

gentle

Comments:

a man who is not quarrelsome

Comments:

a man who is not a lover of money or greedy for gain

Comments:

upright

Comments:

one who desires to be an Elder

Comments:

able to teach

Comments:

able to hold firmly to the trustworthy word

Comments:

able to instruct in sound doctrine

Comments:

able to rebuke those who teach bad doctrine

THE INTERNAL QUALIFICATIONS OF AN ELDER

Comments:

> **SCRIPTURE MEMORIZATION**
> but in your hearts honor Christ the Lord as holy, always being prepared to make a defense to anyone who asks you for a reason for the hope that is in you; yet do it with gentleness and respect,
> *1 Peter 3:15*

SECTION 5

Essentials For The Elder: The Authority Of Scripture

Just in case you haven't understood by this point in the curriculum, let me state the obvious. Should you become an Elder in the church of Jesus Christ, your responsibility and role will be to lead others into a deeper relationship with Jesus Christ. The people under your care will need to be taught and continually guided in how to pray, how to study the Bible, how to understand and apply the scriptures, and how to grow in their devotion and love for Jesus. If you are going to provide that kind of ongoing instruction for the people within your church family, it assumes something very important. *You* must be consistently moving into deeper relationship with Jesus Christ. In other words, *you must know how to shepherd your own soul before you will be able to shepherd others*.

My hope is that you are well on your way in this area. As one who aspires to the role of Elder you need to understand that daily time in the scriptures and a regular habit of prayer are essential for Christian leaders. They are your spiritual food and drink... things you can't do without, like oxygen. They sustain you day after day as you journey toward eternity. I've included these last sections in your training with the prayerful hope that through them you will be better equipped to develop personal habits of your own that work out your salvation (*Philippians 2:12*), resulting in spiritual maturity (*Colossians 1:28,29*).

Q & A

118. Assess your own relationship with Jesus. Is it real? Is it vibrant? Is it ongoing?

119. Do you feel ready to lead other adults spiritually?

120. If not, what steps do you need to take to improve in that?

For the disciple of Jesus Christ, there is no greater earthly resource to provide ongoing growth and maturity than the scriptures of the Old and New Testament. The Bible is God's revelation of Himself and His plan for the redemption of mankind. It is a God-given, amazing resource for our eternal support and spiritual health. As an Elder, the Bible will be your primary source for every bit of wisdom that you are able to instill in the lives of those you lead.

Think about that carefully. The people you may one day lead don't need your dazzling philosophical theories or psychological phrases. They don't need home-spun wisdom or common-sense leadership. They need to hear from God, and God alone. The *Bible* is your primary source of wisdom, as a man and as a potential shepherd of God's people. Without the wisdom that only comes from scripture, you will be in over your head if you attempt to counsel people in the problems and needs of life. In view of that reality, it is vital that you have a firm grasp of the Bible for yourself.

Verbal Plenary Inspiration

Since the Bible is such a vital source of godly instruction and wisdom, it is important that you understand where the Bible came from and why it is so trustworthy. Not only do **you** need to know it, but the people of your church need to know it too. The origin and dependability of the scriptures is foundational to every Christian doctrine and belief, which brings us to the first important doctrine regarding the scriptures, ***the doctrine of inspiration***. For our purposes we are going to expand the definition of inspiration a bit to make very clear what is meant. We'll be talking about the *verbal plenary inspiration* of the scriptures.

> INSPIRATION: When we speak of inspiration, we are referring to the fact that God Himself gave the scriptures to man, in exactly the form He wanted us to have them. That means that the Bible is not a man-made set of documents (contrary to many arguments you will hear) but is divine in origin. Inspiration means that the Bible came from God.
>
> VERBAL: When we say that the Bible is "verbally" inspired we mean that God gave the very words of the Bible to us. Not just the concepts – not just the ideas – the very words. Verbal inspiration insists that God had an intended purpose for what He wanted to communicate and ***did*** communicate it in a way that was intentional and specific, right down to the words He used and the way He used them.
>
> PLENARY: The word "plenary" means, *full* or *complete*. So, when we say the Bible is a book of "Plenary Inspiration" we are saying that all of it, from Genesis to Revelation is inspired of God.
>
> THEREFORE... VERBAL PLENARY INSPIRATION means...
>
> **The entire Bible and every phrase in it, is a product of God's revelation to mankind.**
>
> *Three Things Inspiration does NOT mean...*[3]
>
> 1. Inspiration does ***not*** mean that the Lord mechanically dictated the Bible word-for-word to the human authors without any use or consideration of their human personalities. Theologian B.B. Warfield says, "*If God wished to give His people a series of letters like Paul's, He prepared a Paul to write them, and the Paul He*

---

[3] Concepts here are taken from - Bruce, Packer, Comfort, & Henry, *Origin of the Bible*, (Tyndale House, 2004)

brought to the task was a Paul who spontaneously would write just such letters."[4]
2. Inspiration does **not** mean that any human mistakes made in the transmission of the Bible from the originals to the various copies were inspired as well. Inspiration only applies to the original text.
3. Inspiration does not mean that the Bible is on par with other types of literature that are described as "inspired." When Christians speak of the inspiration of the Bible, they are referring to its divine origin, not the quality of its writing (though the great quality of the biblical writings do naturally flow from its divine origin.)

Biblical Support for the Idea of Inspiration

The Bible itself attests to its divine origin – which we will see in the following passages of scripture...

*"Brothers, the Scripture had to be fulfilled, which the Holy Spirit spoke beforehand by the mouth of David concerning Judas, who became a guide to those who arrested Jesus. - **Acts 1:16***

- Peter says the source of David's written words was the Holy Spirit

*And we have something more sure, the prophetic word, to which you will do well to pay attention as to a lamp shining in a dark place, until the day dawns and the morning star rises in your hearts, knowing this first of all, that no prophecy of Scripture comes from someone's own interpretation. For no prophecy was ever produced by the will of man, but men spoke from God as they were carried along by the Holy Spirit. - **2 Peter 1: 19-21***

- Peter characterizes the "*prophetic word*" (his teaching received from the Holy Spirit) as something "*more sure*" than eyewitness accounts of the Father's affirmation of Jesus when He was baptized.
- Peter emphasizes that scripture does not find its origin with man, but with God.
- Peter teaches that though the words of scripture are from God, they were given through men.
- The divine Author of the Bible is shown to be the Holy Spirit, who carried the human authors along to communicate God's intended meaning accurately.

*All Scripture is breathed out by God and profitable for teaching, for reproof, for correction, and for training in righteousness. - **2 Timothy 3:16***
- Paul teaches Timothy (and us) that scripture is actually "*breathed out*" by God – again emphasizing the divine source of scripture.

---

[4] B. B Warfield, *The Inspiration and Authority of the Bible*, (P & R Publishing, 1948)

- Paul also shows that because the words of scripture come from God Himself, they are profitable to be used in many different ways in the training of God's people.

Q & A

121. Define what is meant by "verbal plenary inspiration."

122. Why is it important to know that the Bible is inspired?

123. What difference does inspiration make to our understanding and application of what the Bible teaches?

124. How does KNOWING that scripture is inspired of God effect your confidence when you think about shepherding others according to what the Bible says?

Who Put the Bible Together?

The Bible has not always been compiled and organized in the form we have today. In fact, there was not a book known as "the Bible" until after the Council of Trent in the 1500s. So how do we know that the scriptures we have really belong in the Bible? And doesn't the Catholic version have extra books? What about those? In this section we'll quickly walk through how the Bible was compiled in the way it was.

The term used to refer to the process of putting the Bible together is "canonization." The word "canon" actually means, "measuring rod, or rule." The process of canonization was the process of determining what books belonged in the Bible and what books did not. Ultimately, it was God who decided what books belong in the Bible. He did so by inspiring its writing in the first place, and only later by having it compiled into one book that we call the Bible, through the various scholars and councils.

The first attempts at compiling biblical books took place in regard to the Old Testament. That process was relatively simple compared to the New Testament, perhaps in part because of the spiritual nature and history of the Jewish people. Jewish rabbis and scholars mainly turned to recognized spiritual leaders (prophets & primary figures in their history) to seek the writings that belonged in their scriptures. While there was some debate in regard to the Old Testament canon, by A.D. 250 there was nearly universal agreement on the canon of Hebrew Scripture.

For the New Testament, the process of the recognition and collection of the scriptures began in the late first century. We can see in the New Testament writings themselves that very early on, some of the New Testament books were being recognized as scripture. For example, Paul considered Luke's writings to be as authoritative as the Old Testament (*1 Timothy 5:18*), and Peter refers to Paul's writings as "scripture" (*2 Peter 3:15-16*). In addition to that, some of the early Christian scholars began to form opinions as to what writings were actually New Testament scripture. For example, Clement of Rome mentioned at least eight New Testament books (A.D. 95). Ignatius of Antioch, about seven books (A.D. 115), Polycarp, a disciple of John the Apostle, acknowledged 15 books (A.D. 108), Irenaeus mentioned 21 books (A.D. 185), and.

ESSENTIALS FOR THE ELDER: THE AUTHORITY OF SCRIPTURE

Hippolytus recognized 22 books (A.D. 170-235).

So how did these varied opinions about what books should be included in the New Testament become reconciled? Various church councils over the years made attempts at compiling a canon of scripture, and in the end the following principles were used in making their determination of what should be considered scripture and what should not. Each document being considered was judged by these criteria.

1) *Was the author an Apostle or did the author have a close connection with an Apostle?*

We can see that any scripture that was actually written by an Apostle of Jesus would have more authority than others, as well as a greater likelihood of being inspired. But there were other authors, like Luke and Mark, who were not Apostles themselves, but were close associates of the Apostles. It was assumed that the writing of men such as this came from first-hand accounts, received from the Apostles themselves. This was a very important consideration to the church councils.

2) *Is the book being accepted by the body of Christ at large?*

In other words, did the people of the church, the body of Christ see the letter or book in question as bearing the mark of divine authority? If so, then it was a likely candidate for inclusion in the canon. If not, it was rejected.

3) *Did the book contain consistency of doctrine and orthodox teaching?*

This point is vital. No book could be included in the Bible if it contradicted other, already-recognized teachings. God, being a God of truth, does not and would not contradict Himself. Any book that taught false or misleading doctrines were not considered for inclusion in the canon.

4) *Did the book bear evidence of high moral and spiritual values that would reflect a work of the Holy Spirit?*

In other words, did the writing have the mark of divine inspiration? Was its content or teaching of the quality and nature that it could have been inspired of God? Many books were rejected from the canon on the basis of these types of questions, and many others were included because of it.

Again, it is very important to remember that the church did not *determine* the canon to be inspired. Their task was to attempt *to recognize what was already inspired* so that those writings could be compiled into one collection – the Bible. In this way, it was God, and God alone, who determined which books belonged in the Bible.

Q & A

125. Take a moment to look over the criteria used to recognize those books that were

inspired of God. Explain how you see them being helpful.

126. Do you understand why the various councils did not *determine* what was scripture, but instead were seeking to *recognize* what was scripture?

Inerrancy

Inerrancy is another of the doctrines that supports the authority of the Bible. Inerrancy is the belief that when correctly interpreted, the Bible is entirely true and never false in what it affirms, in every area to which it speaks. In other words, there are no mistakes or errors in the Bible as it was originally given.

You may have noticed how carefully that was said. That is because it is important to understand that it is only the original manuscripts of the Bible that can properly be said to be inerrant. That is because the Bible was copied by hand from the originals to second and third generation copies (and on and on until our day). "By hand" means that any copies made were made without the benefit of photocopiers. It is entirely possible that some mistakes were made in the copying. In fact, we know this to be the case. As scholars examine the tens of thousands of copies of the scriptures that have been discovered by archaeologists, they find that there are numerous copies that do not read exactly the same, demonstrating that such mistakes were indeed made.

That may sound alarming to you... that the scriptures we have today contain some "mistakes." But rest easy, there is no cause for concern. We are still able to trust the Bible entirely. Why? We can be confident that the Bibles we have today are 98% accurate because so many copies of the scriptures have been found (over 24,000 of the New Testament[5]). What does that have to do with it? Having so many copies available, we are able to compare them with each other. When we do, we quickly see that the vast majority of those documents are consistent with each other, which shows us that the biblical text has been transmitted consistently throughout the ages.

Comparing the copies like this also enables us to identify the few mistakes that do exist – giving us the opportunity to correct them when possible, or at least make note of them as possible copying errors. But the most important thing about these "mistakes" is that none of them has ever had any bearing on a major area of doctrine or belief. In fact, the great majority of them are very minor mistakes that don't impact the meaning of the text at all. For example, some manuscripts may read, "Jesus Christ" while others read, "Christ Jesus." While it is clear that a difference exists, it is also equally clear that the intended meaning remains unchanged.

You should also have noticed that the definition of inerrancy states that "when properly interpreted" the Bible will be found to be entirely true and never false in all it affirms. Why is it said that way? Because people *will* make mistakes in understanding the scriptures... you can count on it. But that does not mean that the scriptures themselves are not trustworthy. Any interpretation or understanding of the scriptures that is opposed to the clear sense of any other scriptural passage does not necessarily imply that the biblical text is in error. In that case the

---

[5] Josh McDowell, *Evidence That Demands A Verdict, Volume I*, (Thomas Nelson, 1993), p. 42-43

interpretation is at fault, not the scripture. One of the earliest Christian scholars, Augustine, made the point that as human beings, we are not allowed to say of any biblical book, "The author of this book is mistaken." Should we ever think that to be the case, Augustine said there is one or more of 3 other issues at work in that situation: 1) the **copy** of the original is faulty, 2) the **translation** of the original is wrong, or 3) you have not understood.[6]

Finally, there are cases of what is called "phenomenological language" in the Bible. That means that the Bible, like most literary works, sometimes speaks in ways that the readers can easily understand rather than in strictly factual terms. One easy example of this is found in Psalm 113:3. *"From the rising of the sun to its setting, the name of the LORD is to be praised!"* We know from modern science that the sun doesn't actually rise or set, but rather that the earth rotates on its axis, giving the appearance that the sun rises and sets. Does the Bible's use of this kind of language mean that the Bible is in error? Not at all! All it means is that God is smart enough to inspire the human authors to write in ways that all people in all times can understand what He is saying!

There is one more way that your interpretation can make a difference in how you understand the Bible – and that has to do with the type of literature you are reading **within** the pages of the Bible. For example – If you were to begin reading something that was handed to you and it began with, *"Once upon a time..."* - what type of literature would you immediately know you were reading? A fairy tale, or fictional story. Another example: What if you were handed a sheet of paper that began, "Dear John,"? You would know it was a letter... possibly an, "I just want to be friends..." letter. The point? Every **type** of writing has its own characteristics, things that are unique to the kind of literature it is.

But beyond that is this point: the type of literature (or the "genre" of literature – pronounced "zhahn-ruh") that you are reading, will determine much of **how** you understand it. For example, poetry is one genre of literature. What do you know about poetry? It may rhyme, it may use symbolism and imagery, or it may use very extreme or exaggerated wording to make its meaning more powerful. We know these things about poetry, so we don't take everything in a poem to be word-for-word literal. That is very important to know. If you don't, you'll misunderstand some of what is being said by the writer.

How does this apply to the Bible? You have to understand that the Bible is a collection of writings, of many different genres of literature. The Bible contains poetry, history, letters, prophecy, genealogies, and other types of literature. When we open our Bibles to a specific passage, we need to recognize what *type* of literature we are reading so that we can understand or interpret its meaning in a way consistent with that type of literature. If we don't, we'll make some serious mistakes in our interpretation, and possibly be led to believe that the Bible is not inerrant.

For example: Psalm 36:7 says, *"How precious is your steadfast love, O God! The children of mankind take refuge in the shadow of your wings."* If we naively assumed that inerrancy means that every word of the scriptures is to be taken in a very hard, literal way, we would come away from this verse believing that God has wings. But as you can see, that misses the point entirely! The Psalms are songs, poems – and as poems they often use imagery to make their point! This verse draws upon a common image (a mother bird sheltering her chicks) to teach that God shelters and protects mankind. Do you see how the type of literature you read within the

---

[6] St. Augustine, Contra Faustum, Volume XI

Bible has a huge impact on how you understand the passage? So, in order to "properly interpret" scripture, as the definition of inerrancy says we must do, we must take into consideration the kind of literature we are reading within the Bible.

Q & A

127. What do you understand "inerrancy" to mean?

128. Why is it important that we hold the Bible to be inerrant?

129. Do you feel that you understand why the Bible is trustworthy in spite of errors that have been found in some of the copies of the original documents?

130. If a person wrongly interprets a passage of scripture, does that mean that the Bible is not true? Why or why not?

131. List some of the different types of literature that can be found in the Bible.

132. What difference does the type of literature we are reading make to our understanding of the scriptures?

The Sufficiency of Scripture

The last thing we want to consider regarding the Bible is the doctrine of sufficiency. If we consider something to be sufficient, we are saying that it is enough, it is complete. When we say that the scriptures are sufficient, we mean exactly the same thing: the Bible contains everything we need in order to adequately know God, His will for our lives, and His plan of salvation. There are a few places we can see this in the scriptures. Let's look at them.

> *All Scripture is breathed out by God and profitable for teaching, for reproof, for correction, and for training in righteousness, that the man of God may be competent, equipped for every good work. - 2 Timothy 3:16-17*

We've already thought about this verse in light of the inspiration of scripture but look at what it says regarding the sufficiency of scripture. All scripture *is* profitable to us – to the extent of equipping us for *every* good work. There is nothing left for us to figure out, nothing more that we need in order to live a godly life. God, in His grace, has given us His own revelation, His own explanation of what is needed for us to obey Him and love Him – and He has done that through giving us the Bible! Let's look at another passage...

> *His divine power has granted to us all things that pertain to life and godliness, through the knowledge of him who called us to his own glory and excellence*
> *-2 Peter 1:3*

ESSENTIALS FOR THE ELDER: THE AUTHORITY OF SCRIPTURE

Initially, this verse doesn't seem to be talking about the scriptures, does it? But it does. Peter tells us that through the exercise of His divine power, God has given us **all** things that we need in order to live in a godly way. That's good news... but how does it relate the sufficiency of scripture? Peter goes on to tell us the avenue by which God does this. We receive everything we need for life and godliness *"through our knowledge of Him (Jesus) who called us to His own glory and excellence."*

Think about that for a minute. How do we come to have this knowledge of Jesus? Someone may have told us about Him, or taught us about Him...but where did *their* knowledge of Jesus come from? Somewhere back along the line, it had to have come from the scriptures! There is no other source of revelation that clearly and accurately tells us who Jesus is and what He has done for us. It is through the scriptures that God applies His divine power to give us all things that pertain to life and godliness! If we truly believe that the scriptures are sufficient for us... that they tell us everything we need to know about God, ourselves, salvation, and how to obey and please God, what impact will that have on our lives? The implications of it are almost endless, but let's look at one example to get your thinking started – the issue of self-esteem.

Western culture has made the concept of self-esteem into a sacred creed. We are told from a very early age that every personal insecurity, every moral pitfall, and every failing we experience stems from our lack of self-esteem. We simply don't think well enough of ourselves, and as a result, we don't live up to our potential. That's why we feel bad about ourselves, are insecure, feel guilty, etc. If we could only think positively about ourselves, we'd be able to accomplish so much more!

Sounds good – but is it true? When we turn to the Bible, believing it to be authoritative, inerrant, and sufficient, we find a very different conclusion. In the Bible we never find God telling us that we think too little of ourselves. In fact, He repeatedly insists that we think far **too much** of ourselves! The scriptures tell us how terribly wretched we are so that we will be able to see the amazing grace of God's offer of salvation in Christ! But we do feel insecure and guilty, don't we? Yes, that is true for every person on the planet. But why do we feel those things? The Bible says we feel those things because we **are** insecure and guilty. The hard, but compassionate truth that God tells us over and over in the scriptures is that our problem is not a lack of self-esteem, our problem is that we are sinners in need of a Savior – and God has given us the only cure available for that problem in His Son, Jesus.

This is only one example out of hundreds or even thousands of ways that a reliance on the sufficiency of scripture will help us to turn *away* from beliefs or practices that are merely cultural, based on psychological theory, or even occultic in nature (such as the New Age beliefs so prevalent in our culture), and turn *to* the truth God reveals in His word. We are not lacking an adequate revelation of God or His ways. He gave us everything we need in the scriptures.

This truth applies directly to everyday life. In light of this truth, we have much to reconsider, and much repenting to do. One author puts it this way, *"...we do not need to be afraid of 'new' revelations being proposed. We should also repent of our spiritual pragmatism that substitutes 'what works' for what God has said. This applies to everything from the way we approach evangelism and corporate worship, to the means we pursue for spiritual growth, to the way we think about marriage, or work, or parenting, etc."*[7]

---

[7] Stephen A. Welch, "Intro to Systematic Theology/The Doctrine of the Word", (Capitol Hill Baptist Church, Systematic Theology Core Seminar,

Q & A

133. Explain what you understand is meant by "the sufficiency of scripture."

134. Why is it important for us to hold firmly to this truth? What impact will it have on us and the churches we may lead, if we do not?

WRITTEN QUIZ

In the following questions, do your best to answer without reviewing this section. If you have trouble recalling the information, don't worry – you'll discuss your answers with your mentor!

- Explain what is mean by "verbal plenary" inspiration.

- Biblically, where do we get this idea?

- Why is it important to know that the Bible is inspired?

- Briefly explain how the Bible was compiled into the form it is in today.

- What is meant by the term "inerrancy?"

- Why is it important to know the Bible is inerrant?

- What difference does the Bible's trustworthiness make to your life?

- If you become an Elder, what difference will the Bible's trustworthiness make in how you counsel and disciple others?

- What do we mean when we say that the scriptures are sufficient?

- How do these issues relate to knowledge we might gain from other sources, such as science, psychology, business, etc.?

> **SCRIPTURE MEMORIZATION**
>
> *All Scripture is breathed out by God and profitable for teaching, for reproof, for correction, and for training in righteousness, that the man of God may be competent, equipped for every good work.*
> ***2 Timothy 3:16-17***

SECTION 6

Essentials For The Elder: Basic Doctrines

Though it is true that every believer is responsible to learn the scriptures and develop their own spiritual walk, those men who become Elders have a particular responsibility to devote additional time and energy to the study of the Word of God. Every Elder has the calling to be responsible for the teaching diet those within the church receive. They are to make sure that the church leadership (the Elder team) is teaching what accords with scripture, and that those within the church are being made aware of teachings outside their local church that are untrue or particularly dangerous.

I have already emphasized that Elders are the doctrinal guardians of the church, and it's quite possible that a job description like that seems overwhelming to you. There is a sense in which it is! For example, exactly what doctrines are Elders supposed to uphold? What beliefs are essential for Christians to maintain? What are the main things the Elder team should be teaching and keeping an eye on? Those are very valid questions... ones that we will be addressing in this section.

While it is true that there are many, many doctrines taught in the Bible, it is also true that there are some of those that serve as foundational teachings, out of which the others flow. The man who serves as an Elder needs to be well-grounded first, in these basics of the Christian faith. He needs to understand clearly who God is (Father, Son, Holy Spirit), how God has revealed Himself to mankind (the person of Jesus), and how human beings are brought into right relationship with God (the gospel message). It is these areas of basic doctrine that inform and impact every other doctrine. A man well-grounded in these areas will be well equipped to serve the church.

God: The Trinity

When I say, "Trinity," I'm referring to the nature in which God exists – as three persons who share one divine essence or being. This concept is one of the most confusing and misunderstood teachings of the Bible, which is ironic since it is one of the most foundational doctrines the Bible teaches! A good part of why it is confusing is because it is a God-sized concept that we are trying to grasp with our human-sized intellects. Said another way, the doctrine of the Trinity doesn't make perfect sense to us. There is truly nothing else we know that is comparable to the nature of the Trinity.

When we speak of the Trinity we are speaking about God – and more precisely, about His nature. That is one of the reasons why it is important to have a right understanding and belief about the Trinity. To believe wrongly on this point, is to believe God to be something that He is not... which will ultimately do us harm, not good. God is who He is – and who He is, is glorious! As His followers we need to do our utmost to worship Him both in spirit, and in truth (*John 4:23*), and we are better able to do so when we understand Him for who He really is.

But there's another important reason to understand the doctrine of the Trinity - each member of the Trinity is intimately involved in God's plan of redemption, and it is to our everlasting joy to understand His work in our salvation as fully as we are able.

Q & A

135. Give some reasons why it is important for us to understand the doctrine of the Trinity?

136. Why is it particularly important for Elders to know?

Trinity: The basic concept

Though the Bible never uses the word "Trinity," it is a concept that is clearly taught throughout the scriptures. There are many, many places in the pages of the Bible where we see God referred to in ways that show us that He is "one" in essence or being, but "three" persons at the same time. It's not that God "shows" or "manifests" Himself in three different forms or ways at various times, it's that God exists eternally and at all times as Father, *and* Son, *and* Holy Spirit. Throughout the ages scholars, Pastors, and theologians have sought helpful ways to describe this concept, though no earthly illustration is up to the challenge! However, there is an ancient diagram which has proven helpful that illustrates the relationships between Father, Son, and Holy Spirit, but also demonstrates their unity.

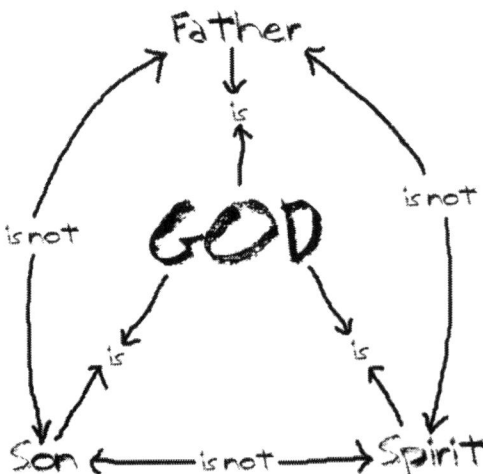

As you can see in the drawing, each of the members of the Trinity *is God* (represented by the lines leading to the center), and at the same time each of the members of the Trinity *is not* the others (represented by the lines connecting between the individual names.) It can be very baffling, until you begin to see how this idea is described in the scriptures. As you notice the details of how God describes His own nature, you start to see that He is a being unlike any other. Instead of me continuing to explain it to you in my own words, let's look at scripture so that you can see the biblical idea of the Trinity for yourself.

Trinity: What the Bible teaches

From the very beginning of the Bible, we see the notion of the Trinity expressed. The first evidence is not obvious to those of us who do not read Hebrew (the language the Old Testament was written in) but is important to consider. The very first verse of the Bible states, *"In the beginning, God created the heavens and the earth"* (Genesis 1:1).

I want to draw your attention to the word in this sentence that is translated "God." It is the Hebrew word "Elohim." "Elohim" is a *plural* word. That means it refers to *more than one*. Just like we add an "s" or "es" to a word in English in order to make it refer to more than one, the Hebrew language adds "im" to words in order to make them refer to more than one. The point of *this* verse using *this* particular word is not that there were multiple gods who created the heavens and earth, but that God Himself is "more than one," a tri-unity (Trinity). Of course, this verse alone does not make it clear that there are three persons in the Trinity, but it does begin the Bible with a clear "hint" at that truth.

In the same chapter of Genesis, we see another significant hint of the triune nature of God, spoken by God Himself. Genesis chapter 1, verse 26 says, *"Then God said, 'Let us make man in our image, after our likeness. And let them have dominion over the fish of the sea and over the birds of the heavens and over the livestock and over all the earth and over every creeping thing that creeps on the earth.'"* Did you notice how God said, *"Let **us**"* and *"in **our** image"* and *"in **our** likeness*?"

There have been many attempts at explaining this odd word usage, apart from the idea of the Trinity. Some say God was speaking in what is known as a "royal plural," which kings are known to do from time to time as a sign of their position and authority. While it would certainly be true that as the ultimate authority God could rightly speak that way, it is not a form of speech that was common in the day or culture in which the Old Testament was written. For that reason, it doesn't seem satisfactory to accept it as the right explanation.

Others have proposed that when God said, *"us"* He was referring to Himself and to the angelic beings who were with Him. This suggestion may sound possible initially, but a closer look at the text shows this cannot be the case. Look again at the verse. It says, *"'Let us make man in our image, after our likeness...'"* The word *"us"* is obviously plural (referring to more than one), but the words *"image"* and *"likeness"* are singular (referring to only one). In other words, God did *not* say, "Let us make man in our images, in our likenesses," which He would say if He were referring to others in addition to Himself. But that's not how He said it. He was clearly only referring to one image or likeness – thus only one being.

In addition, God can't be talking about other beings like angels who are alongside Him... because they don't share the same "image" or "likeness" as God. That becomes even more obvious when we follow the thought into the next verse. Genesis 1:27, *"So God created man in his own image, in the image of God he created him; male and female he created them."* This verse shows very clearly that the only image in mind is the image or likeness of God, who must be the "*us*" referred to in the previous verse.

In addition, the Bible never indicates that angelic beings had any part in the creation of the heavens and earth... but it *does* tell us that Jesus played a part in creation! Look at these verses...

> *He (Jesus) is the image of the invisible God, the firstborn of all creation. For by him all things were created, in heaven and on earth, visible and invisible, whether thrones or dominions or rulers or authorities--all things were created through him and for him.* - **Colossians 1:15-16**

> *Long ago, at many times and in many ways, God spoke to our fathers by the prophets, but in these last days he has spoken to us by his Son, whom he appointed the heir of all things, through whom also he created the world.* - **Hebrews 1:1-2**

These New Testament verses help us understand who the "*us*" was in Genesis chapter 1! Jesus was there, as part of the Trinity, involved in the beginning moments of the earth's creation. Reading a bit farther in Genesis 1, we see the Holy Spirit present, *"The earth was without form and void, and darkness was over the face of the deep. And the Spirit of God was hovering over the face of the waters."* The Father, the Son, and the Holy Spirit were all active participants in the creation of the heavens and earth – and can rightly be seen as the "*us*" who are referred to in the Genesis account.

Another place we see "*us*" used in reference to God is in Genesis 11:7-8. This passage recounts the building of the tower at Babel, where God said, *"Come, let us go down and there confuse their language, so that they may not understand one another's speech. So, the LORD dispersed them from there over the face of all the earth, and they left off building the city."*

Notice that again God refers to Himself in a plural sense (us). He says that this "*us*" is going to confuse the language of the people. Then, as we see that action take place, we are told that *"the LORD"* is the one who did it. In this context it is equally clear, the "*us*" refers to God alone. These two examples from the beginning pages of the Bible show us hints of the idea of the Trinity.

Q & A

137. How does the word usage itself show that God was not speaking to angelic beings when He said, "Let us..."?

Isaiah chapter 6 gives the account of the prophet Isaiah's vision of the Lord. The Lord was seated on His throne in great glory. Speaking to Isaiah, God uses the word "*us*" to refer to Himself. Isaiah 6:8 - *"And I heard the voice of the Lord saying, 'Whom shall I send, and who will go for us?' Then I said, 'Here am I! Send me.'"* Here God refers to Himself by using both "*I*" and "*us*." His own reference to Himself shows us both the unity and the diversity within the Trinity. And in keeping with the way the word "*us*" is used in the Genesis accounts, it makes perfect sense that the Lord was talking about Himself.

Isaiah 61:1 also gives us a very revealing glimpse into the existence of and relationships within the Trinity. Notice what it says, *"The Spirit of the Lord God is upon me, because the LORD has anointed me to bring good news to the poor; he has sent me to bind up the brokenhearted, to proclaim liberty to the captives, and the opening of the prison to those who are bound; to proclaim the year of the LORD's favor..."*

Clearly there are two members of the Trinity (Father and Spirit) present and active in this situation, but we must be careful to notice that a third member of the Trinity (Jesus) is also present. He is the one speaking! How do we know this? Because in Luke Chapter 4, Jesus finds and reads this exact passage of scripture in a public gathering at the synagogue and ***claims that it refers to Himself***! His exact words are found in Luke 4:21 - *And he began to say to them, "Today this Scripture has been fulfilled in your hearing."*

Q & A

138. What importance do the New Testament's remarks about the Old Testament have to do with issues like this?

Up to this point we've looked mainly at Old Testament passages, of which there are still many more we could consider. But for the sake of time let's turn to the New Testament to see how it presents this idea of the Trinity.

First, we find all three members of the Trinity spoken of and present at the baptism of Jesus. Matthew 3:16-17 - *"And when Jesus was baptized, immediately he went up from the water, and behold, the heavens were opened to him, and he saw the Spirit of God descending like a dove and coming to rest on him; and behold, a voice from heaven said, 'This is my beloved Son, with whom I am well pleased.'"*

Did you notice the Son (Jesus) is baptized, the Father speaks an affirmation of Him, and the Spirit descends on Him? These verses do not tell us that all three are equally God, but it does show all three together, which means that they cannot be differing manifestations or modes of one God. If that were the case, then they could not all 3 be present at once. It is clear that each of them is a separate and distinct person.

At the end of Matthew's gospel, Jesus gives His disciples instructions about what they should do once He returns to Heaven. Here's what He says, *" All authority in heaven and on earth has been given to me. Go therefore and make disciples of all nations, baptizing them in the name of the Father and of the Son and of the Holy Spirit, teaching them to observe all that I have commanded you. And behold, I am with you always, to the end of the age"* (*Matthew 28:18-20*).

The important thing to notice is how Jesus says this baptism is to take place. People are to be baptized in the name (singular) of the Father, and of the Son, and of the Holy Spirit (plural – 3 persons). The way it is worded, all three are considered to be known by the same name. What name would that be? Yahweh, the name of God Himself (*Exodus 3:14*). All three persons make up one God. Though each is clearly different in His personality and role, all three persons are "one" in their divinity - three, co-equal members of the God-head: Father, Son, Holy Spirit.

We also see John's testimony about Jesus clearly declaring Him to be divine. John chapter 1 contains many key verses that show Jesus being God...

In the beginning was the Word, and the Word was with God, and the Word was God. He was in the beginning with God. All things were made through him, and without him was not any thing made that was made. - **John 1:1-3**

And the Word became flesh and dwelt among us, and we have seen his glory, glory as of the only Son from the Father, full of grace and truth. (John bore witness about him, and cried out, "This was he of whom I said, 'He who comes after me ranks before me, because he was before me.'") And from his fullness we have all received, grace upon grace. For the law was given through Moses; grace and truth came through Jesus Christ. No one has ever seen God; the only God, who is at the Father's side, he has made him known. - **John 1:14-18**

The "Word" spoken of in verse 1 was both **with** God and **was** God in the beginning. Again, we see that they are one, but distinct. In verse 14 we see that this "Word" became flesh and lived among us as a human being, in the person of Jesus. And finally, the last sentence of these verses tells us that Jesus *is* the only God, who is at the Father's side. Once more, we see both Father and Son referred to as God, yet also considered to be distinct from one another.

Q & A

139. Write out some of your thoughts about John chapter 1 in relation to how it speaks of Jesus as God.

140. What difference does it make to *you* to know that the man Jesus is also God?

You might hear the claim from time to time that Jesus never claimed to be God, but people who say such things simply aren't being honest with the scriptures. On a number of occasions Jesus asserted His divinity. One of those times is recorded for us in John chapter 8.

Jesus was being questioned by the religious leaders of His day, and they weren't very happy with what they were hearing. They did not believe Jesus to be the Messiah, and they did not believe Him to be God. The statement that brought the conversation to an abrupt halt comes in verse 56. *"'Your father Abraham rejoiced that he would see my day. He saw it and was glad.' So, the Jews said to him, 'You are not yet fifty years old, and have you seen Abraham?' Jesus said to them, 'Truly, truly, I say to you, before Abraham was, I am.' So, they picked up stones to throw at him, but Jesus hid himself and went out of the temple."*

What did Jesus say that made them so angry that they wanted to kill Him? Two things, both which make the case for Him being God in the flesh... First, He declared Himself to have existed before Abraham (who lived approximately 2000 years prior to Jesus' earthly birth). That could not be true if He were not eternal. Secondly, He intentionally refers to Himself by using the very name of God revealed to Moses (*Exodus 3:14*), "I AM." Their hostile reaction shows that they did not misunderstand His meaning... because anyone who claimed to be God could be killed under the Jewish law. Jesus clearly claimed to be God.

ESSENTIALS FOR THE ELDER: BASIC DOCTRINES

Q & A

141. Explain what Jesus was saying about Himself in John 8:56.

142. Does it seem clear to you that Jesus was claiming to be God?

We also see the Holy Spirit clearly indicated to be God in Acts chapter 5. In that situation, a man (Ananias) and his wife (Sapphira) had sold some land and were donating some of the proceeds of the land sale to the work of the Lord through the ministry of the new-born church. But they told the church leaders that they were donating *all* of the money they had made. In other words, they lied about the amount of money they were giving, apparently so that others would think well of them.

The Lord took this very seriously, and Peter, one the first leaders of the new church confronted them. It is Peter's words to Ananias we are most interested in... Acts 5:3-4 - *"But Peter said, 'Ananias, why has Satan filled your heart to lie to the Holy Spirit and to keep back for yourself part of the proceeds of the land? While it remained unsold, did it not remain your own? And after it was sold, was it not at your disposal? Why is it that you have contrived this deed in your heart? You have not lied to men but to God.'"*

Did you see it? First Peter said that Ananias had lied to the Holy Spirit, then he said that his lie was really against God. In Peter's mind, the Holy Spirit was as much God as the Father or the Son. This is one of the clearest places we see the Holy Spirit as a member of the Trinity.

Q & A

143. Why do you think this couple's lying was such a big deal? Does it have anything to do with what we are considering in this chapter?

In the following chart, you'll see a list of descriptions on the left hand side. In the columns to the right, you will see scriptural passages where each of the members of the Trinity is described by that description. Start at the top of the chart, moving right to left across each row, and look up the scriptures to see for yourself that the Bible describes each of the members of the Trinity in terms that can only be used of God.

Common Characteristics of the Members of the Trinity

	FATHER	SON	SPIRIT
Is called God	Philippians 1:2	John 1:1,14	Acts 5:3-4
Is said to resurrect	1 Thessalonians 1:10	John 2:19, 10:17	Romans 8:11
Indwells believers	2 Corinthians 6:16	Colossians 1:27	John 14:17
Is everywhere	1 Kings 8:27	Matthew 28:20	Psalm 139:7-10
Is all knowing	1 John 3:20	John 16:30, 21:17	1 Corinthians 2:9-11

Sanctifies people	1 Thessalonians 5:23	Hebrews 2:11	1 Peter 1:2
Is a life-giver	Genesis 2:7	John 1:3, 5:21	2 Corinthians 3:6,8
Fellowships with us	1 John 1:3	1 Corinthians 1:9	2 Corinthians 13:14
Is eternal	Psalm 90:2	Micah 5:1-2	Romans 8:11
Has a will	Luke 22:42	Luke 22:42	1 Corinthians 12:11
Speaks	Matthew 3:17	Luke 5:20	Acts 8:29, 11:12
Loves	John 3:16	Ephesians 5:25	Romans 15:30
Searches hearts	Jeremiah 17:10	Revelation 2:23	1 Corinthians 2:10

To wrap up this defense of the triune nature of God consider this. It has been noted by some scholars that the statement that *"God is love"* made in 1 John 4, verses 8 and 16, could not be true if God did not exist as Trinity. Do you understand what they mean?

What they are saying is that love is a relational term. In order for love to exist it requires that there be at least two individuals involved. First, love cannot be expressed (and likely would not exist at all) if there is nothing or no one to love (an object of the love). Second, love cannot be given if there is not one who gives it.

God could not be love, in His very essence as these verses say, if He only existed as one person. This idea becomes clearer when we consider that God is eternal – has no beginning and no end (*Genesis 1:1, John 1:1*). He has always existed. Connect that to the idea that *"God is love."* How could God exist eternally, before any other beings existed, *as love*, if He did not exist as more than one in His own nature? There would be no other person to love, so God could not rightly be said to *be* love.

Q &A

144. In your own words, explain how God actually "being" love means that there has to have always been multiple persons within His being.

Why does it matter?

You may be wondering if all this verbal hair-splitting really has much significance. It can be very difficult at first to see what relevance the doctrine of the Trinity has on everyday life. But rest assured, there are some very practical things that flow out of your beliefs about the nature of God. Let's take a quick look at a few of those...

It's all about the relationship

One of the most significant aspects of any relationship is getting to know who the other person *is*. You want to know who they are, so that you can understand them and therefore love them better. Think about your closest human relationship. Maybe it's the relationship you enjoy with your wife (*if you are married, I would hope so!*). When you consider all the different things about your wife that make her who she is, do you ever ask, "Why does it matter?" or "What benefit does this have for me?"

For example: She is female. Are you deeply concerned about *why* her being female matters to you? Not usually. You simply accept that she is female as a fact of who she is, and you live and relate with her in light of that fact. You enjoy that fact plenty, but you seldom spend time asking, "Why does it matter to me?" To treat your relationship with your wife in that way is to view your relationship in utilitarian, pragmatic terms instead of relational terms. That's not what relationships are about or for. Relationships are about knowing the other person and valuing them for who they are, so that you can understand and love them better.

When it comes to knowing that God exists as Trinity, the same issue is front and center. It's almost **entirely** about the relationship you have with Him. Understanding the nature of the Trinity (as much as you are able), enables you to better know God, to appreciate the multi-faceted reality of who He is. That in turn enables you to love Him more **because** of who He is.

Grasping the concept of the Trinity fills your heart with wonder, awe, and gratitude that you are able to know something of this infinite, complex God. It amazes you that He has revealed Himself to you in such a deeply intimate way. He's shown you aspects of His very nature that you would otherwise have never known.

Q &A

145. Explain your own understanding of how the knowledge of the Trinity has more to do with relationship than anything else.

146. How does that impact your approach to understanding and appreciating the doctrine of the Trinity?

The Trinity impacts how you view life

Beliefs matter. They are the unspoken "rules" that ultimately determine how we behave and interact with others. Whether or not you believe in the Trinity is one of those underlying beliefs that **will** have an impact on your life. For example – someone who believes that "all is one," or "all is god," is called a Pantheist. They believe that this "god" that makes up all that exists has always existed and is nothing more than an impersonal force... ("use the force Luke"). Sound familiar?

The impersonal nature of the Pantheistic "god" provides no basis for ideas of right and wrong, or compassion and love, because it is an impersonal power that does not contain any such distinctions. In addition, the Pantheist's view cannot be harmonized with the actual world we live in. In other words, a Pantheist who is true to his convictions can have no place for individual people or things. He has no reason to distinguish between himself and me, or you, or a tree, or a rock. It's all "one" to him. He cannot answer whether a human being is more important or valuable than a rock, ant, or bacteria. Do you see that what you believe about the very nature of God makes a difference in how you view life?

Another way of looking at the world is what we might call a Naturalist. The Naturalist (which most Atheists are, by the way) would say that matter has always existed. It is only by chance and some misunderstood processes of nature that everything has evolved into what it is today (they call it "natural selection"). So again, we have an impersonal force, but this time much more random, that serves as the ultimate "truth" of the universe.

Unlike the Pantheist, the Naturalist has no problem accepting the world as it is. In fact, he'll try to explain *why* it is like it is, using scientific theories and methods. But the Naturalist will naturally come up short when pressed to explain "why" the universe holds together as it does. In the end, the Naturalist must rely on random chance to explain everything, which gives absolutely no meaning to life whatsoever. In such a view, people are nothing more than cogs in a cosmic machine with little to no significance – no more important than a single-cell organism, or even a speck of dirt.

But thankfully, there is another option through which we can view the world, one based on truth. It is called Theism. The Theist believes that a personal, Creator exists, and out of nothing He created all that is. In this view, the creation itself has meaning, as does history, time, and human life. The complexity of the created realm points to the Creator who made it, demonstrating His power, wisdom, and sovereignty (*Psalm 19*).

Taking it a step farther, there is another kind of theist, a Trinitarian Theist (one who believes that the Creator-God of theism exists as Trinity). This is the view I'm teaching you, and that the Bible supports. This is the only option that can explain both the one (God) and the many (everything else), while saying that people are important at the same time.

In Trinitarian Theism, God Himself is the eternal, infinite reference point for His creation. He is the standard for right and wrong. Who He is determines the "rules" of nature and existence. When we seek to understand the concept of the Trinity, we can understand how the created realm is full of amazing diversity yet can still be unified in a clock-work precision that actually works. It is an out-growth of the Triune God who created it... He is one God who exists in a plural unity. Do you see how what you believe about God really does have a lot to do with how you see the world?

Q & A

147. Explain how your view of God impacts the way you view the world and life in it.

148. How does belief in the Trinity make sense of the world as it is?

The Trinity provides your salvation

We're about to wade into some pretty deep waters, but I believe that with the Spirit's help you can follow along. The amazing mystery of our salvation through Jesus is something we gladly receive but sadly don't give a lot of thought to. But if we take the time to think about it more carefully, we will begin to see that in doing so we can more fully appreciate it, and better know the amazing nature of the God who provides it for us.

Our salvation centers around the character of God. Who He is has to do with both the need for salvation and how we receive it. What do I mean by that? To begin with we must understand that whatever God is, He is perfectly. So, He is perfect in His love. He is perfect in

His justice. He is perfect in His mercy. He is perfect in His holiness...and on the list goes. The point is that were God less than perfect in any of His characteristics, He would not *be* God.

Moving on from there, let's consider the 4 qualities of God we just mentioned, and how they relate to our salvation. God is perfectly *holy, just, merciful,* and *loving.* It is the holiness (purity) of God that makes our sin so offensive and terrible. Because He is *holy,* He cannot and will not put up with our sinful condition or our sinful actions. If He did, He would not be God.

But more than that, His perfect *justice* demands that the offense of our sin be made right. Just as we demand a murderer "pay for his crime," so God demands that we pay for ours (sin). If He did not, He would not be God. Those two qualities of God, in all their perfection, set the stage for our salvation by identifying us as sinners and requiring that our sins be held to account.

But there is more to God than simply those two qualities. There is also His perfect *love* and His perfect *mercy.* Because of His perfect *love,* God desires for us to be redeemed, to be made right with Him so that there is no longer any offense between us because of our sinful condition and sinful actions. That love prompts His perfect *mercy* to provide a way for our redemption to occur. If He did not take this step, He would not be God.

This is where God being "Trinity" comes into the picture of our salvation. It is out of God's triune nature that salvation is at all possible. Why? Because He would be unable to be both the holy judge who meets out our sentence **and** the merciful justifier who pays the price for it in a substitutionary way, if He were not more than one person. Stay with me now...

If God showed us love and mercy, resulting in our forgiveness, *without* some kind of payment for it, then He would be violating His own perfect holiness and justice. That can't happen, or else He would not be God. If on the other hand, He exercised His holy justice toward us, resulting in our condemnation, *without* expressing His love and mercy, then He would be violating His own perfect love and mercy. That can't happen either, or else He would not be God.

This is where the Trinity comes to the rescue. Because God is triune, three persons in one co-eternal, co-divine union, He is able to be **both** the judge and the justifier.... and that's exactly what the scriptures tell us happened.

> *...for all have sinned and fall short of the glory of God, and are justified by his grace as a gift, through the redemption that is in Christ Jesus, whom God put forward as a propitiation by his blood, to be received by faith. This was to show God's righteousness, because in his divine forbearance he had passed over former sins. It was to show his righteousness at the present time, so that he might be just and the justifier of the one who has faith in Jesus.* -**Romans 3:23-26**

Let's walk through it slowly and carefully. God the Father, in His perfect holiness, justly declares that we fall short of His glory because of our sinful condition and acts. But in His divine love and mercy, He sends His Son Jesus to be our justifier, taking our place, receiving the punishment that was due us. It is through the work of the Trinity, that our salvation is even possible.

So far, we've seen that the Father exercises His just judgment toward our sin, but in His love He sends Jesus to express His mercy by being our Justifier. But the transaction is not complete. Those two acts don't automatically give us God's forgiveness. We must trust in Jesus to receive it, and that's where the Holy Spirit comes in. It's the Holy Spirit who awakens us from spiritual death so that we are able to respond in faith. John chapter three is the best place for us to see this...

In answering some questions about how a person becomes "born again" Jesus says in verses 6-8, " *'Truly, truly, I say to you, unless one is born of water and the Spirit, he cannot enter the kingdom of God. That which is born of the flesh is flesh, and that which is born of the Spirit is spirit. Do not marvel that I said to you, "You must be born again." The wind blows where it wishes, and you hear its sound, but you do not know where it comes from or where it goes. So, it is with everyone who is born of the Spirit.'* "

Jesus said that being saved, being born again, is the same as being "*born of the Spirit.*" It is the Spirit who gives spiritual birth to us, who brings us to new life. Just like you didn't cause yourself to be physically born, you don't cause yourself to be spiritually born. The Holy Spirit is the Father's agent who causes us to awaken to our need for God's salvation and to accept the love of God given to us through Jesus Christ.

Again, in John 6:63 Jesus says, "*It is the Spirit who gives life; the flesh is no help at all.*" Romans 8:15 says, "*For you did not receive the spirit of slavery to fall back into fear, but you have received the Spirit of adoption as sons, by whom we cry, 'Abba! Father!'* " It is the Spirit of God that adopts us into the family of God, bringing forgiveness and salvation. 1 Corinthians 6:11 tells us, "*And such were some of you. But you were washed, you were sanctified, you were justified in the name of the Lord Jesus Christ and by the Spirit of our God.*" It is the Spirit who brings us to salvation. The Trinity makes all the difference when it comes to salvation. Without God being triune, we would have no possible hope of forgiveness.

Q & A

149. Explain what is meant when we say God is "Trinity."

150. Give some reasons that it is vital for us to understand and believe that God exists as Trinity.

151. How is our salvation dependent on God existing as Trinity?

Prayer is dependent on the Trinity

We can also see how vital the truth of the Trinity is when we consider how it impacts our prayers. Even our prayers are dependent on God being triune. Our prayers are answered ultimately, by the Father (*Matthew 6:6, Matthew 7:11, John 15:16, John 16:23*). He is the one that we are praying to. But we do the actual praying *through* the authority of the Son, Jesus (*John 15:16*). He is our intercessor, the one who takes our requests to the Father (*Hebrews 10:19-22*). As we pray, we are to pray *in* the Holy Spirit, in His power and with His guidance (*Romans 8:26-27, Ephesians 6:18*). Paul wrote to the Ephesian church, "*For through him we both have access in one Spirit to the Father*" (*Ephesians 2:18*). **Through** Jesus, we have access **in** one Spirit, **to** the Father. The interrelationships of the Trinity are the avenue through which we pray, and by which prayer works as it does.

ESSENTIALS FOR THE ELDER: BASIC DOCTRINES

Q & A

152. Explain how prayer involves every member of the Trinity. Try to talk it out in your own words so that you can understand it more clearly.

What Makes God, God?

That's a pretty amazing question to ponder, isn't it? But it is a very necessary and helpful question. God desires to be known, and our answer to that question will help us to know Him. But let's be careful that we keep the right attitude about it. As God says, *"For as the heavens are higher than the earth, so are my ways higher than your ways and my thoughts than your thoughts."* (*Isaiah 55:9*). We must begin with the humility appropriate to created beings who are seeking to know their Creator. He is above us and beyond us.

In our pursuit of Him there will be many times when our logic and understanding simply aren't adequate. God-sized concepts cannot entirely fit within a human understanding or frame of reference. Are you able to accept that? Can you place your trust in God's word to reveal things *as* true, even if you can't understand *how* they can be true?

Along that line, please understand this: this section is *not* intended to give you a complete understanding of the character of God. That would be like trying to drink the entire Pacific Ocean, using only a thimble! Our puny human minds can't hope to take in all that God is. But we are able to drink in *some* if it – to get a taste, an idea, a better understanding of God and what makes Him God. So, this section *is* intended to be an introductory taste, a beginning look at the vital and important things that make up the character of our great God.

We've already spoken of the mind-boggling concept of the Trinity. We could spend the rest of our lives on that concept alone and never come to a complete understanding of it. But there is more than the concept of the Trinity that can be known about God. His very "God-ness" involves a completeness of being that we humans can't relate to and are hardly able to conceive. But we can know some of it, on some basic levels.

We'll make that beginning by introducing a new term: **attributes**. The attributes of God are the qualities that are *essential* to His nature – the things that, if they were not true of Him, would cause Him to cease to *be* God. As one theologian puts it, *"Every attribute is identical to His being. He is what He has. Whatever God is, He is completely and simultaneously."*[8]

Do you understand what he's saying? It is similar to some of the ideas we covered when speaking of the importance of God being Trinity, as it relates to our salvation. These attributes, or qualities that God possesses, *are* what He *is*. All of them together are what make Him who and what He is. Beyond that, every one of the qualities (attributes) that comprises God's being, are completely perfect in their essence, and exist all at once.

For example: One attribute of God is that He is merciful. So, if God is merciful, then He must be *perfectly* merciful and *completely* merciful in order to *be* God. Another of God's attributes is that He is just. So, being God, His justice is *perfect* and *complete* justice. But His

---

[8] H. Bavinck, *Doctrine of God*, (Grand Rapids, Mich.: Baker, 1951) p. 121

justice is never less complete or perfect than His mercy and His mercy is never less complete or perfect than His justice. So, everything God does, or says, or ordains to occur is done out of the complete perfection of all of His attributes.

Have you blown a mind-gasket yet? As I said, our puny minds can't take it all in, but we can get a taste. The example given above is just one example that relates to two of His attributes. And there are thousands more attributes that make up our God! In a few moments, we will be considering quite a few more of the attributes that are essential to the nature of God. As we do, keep in mind that every one of them is perfect and complete in what it is, and is perfectly related to and interacting with all the other attributes at all times! Tighten down that gasket... here we go!

Communicable Attributes & Incommunicable Attributes

For the sake of having some categories that are helpful in sorting out our understanding of God, theologians have come up with two different ways of describing the various attributes of God: ***communicable attributes*** and ***incommunicable attributes***. In using these two terms, they mean that some of the attributes of God are qualities that He chose to share with human beings when He made us in His image (*Genesis 1:26*). These are the communicable (shared) attributes; things like love, justice, mercy, compassion, etc. They are perfectly true of God, and true of mankind in a less perfect way.

The second category of attributes, the incommunicable ones, are the things that are true of God alone. Nobody on earth, and no part of creation shares these qualities with God; things like omniscience (complete knowledge), omnipresence (being present in every place at once), etc.

Q & A

153. Define what we mean when we speak of God's "attributes."

154. Explain how you understand the complete and simultaneous nature of each of God's attributes. It's tough but do your best!

155. Explain how you understand the difference between incommunicable and communicable attributes.

Aseity - God is self-existent

As we begin to consider the characteristics or qualities that make God, God, we must start here. God is self-existent. He is not dependent on anything or anyone else for His existence. It is determined by Himself alone. This is very hard for us to fully grasp, since we and everything we know has some type of dependence on other things for existence. Our bodies require oxygen, food, proper temperatures, etc. in order to continue existing. Even our soul or spirit does not exist of itself, it was created by God when we were conceived in our mother's womb.

But God is altogether different in that respect. He exists – period. No beginning, and no end. Paul proclaims to the philosophers and men of Athens, *"The God who made the world and everything in it, being Lord of heaven and earth, does not live in temples made by man, nor is he served by human hands, as though he needed anything, since he himself gives to all mankind life and breath and everything*" (Acts 17:25). God Himself doesn't depend on anything for His existence, in fact, He is the source of everything else.

Paul says it another way in Romans 11:36, "*For from him and through him and to him are all things. To him be glory forever. Amen.*" In short, God doesn't need us – we need Him. In fact, God doesn't need anything at all. Instead, everything that is, flows out of His existence. In knowing this, we should be humbled, both at our own insignificance in comparison to God, and that He would care to include us in His plans at all. We should live in continual amazement that the eternal, self-existing Creator-God has chosen to love us and help us. And we should be confident that His purpose for all of history, and our part in it, will be accomplished.

Q & A

156. Tell in your own words what is meant by God's aseity.

157. Is this a communicable or incommunicable attribute

158. What do we learn about ourselves when we understand that God is self-existent?

159. How does it make you feel about God's love for you?

Immutable – God is unchanging

Immutable means that in His nature or character, God never changes. "*Every good gift and every perfect gift is from above, coming down from the Father of lights with whom there is no variation or shadow due to change*" (*James 1:17*). He does not vary or change – He is immutable. God says more clearly in Malachi 3:6, "*For I the LORD do not change.*" The truth of God's immutable nature means that He does not learn, or grow, or improve over time. He is constant, altogether perfect in His being – the same yesterday, today, and forever (*Hebrews 13:8*).

But God is also unchanging in His decrees or purposes. They do not need to change because of His perfection. He does not make mistakes, become surprised by unseen circumstances or events, or ever say, "*Oops!*" Therefore, He has no need to change. The Bible says, "*The counsel of the LORD stands forever, the plans of his heart to all generations.*" (*Psalm 33:11*) This truth is a great comfort to God's people. We can trust Him, completely. There is never a reason to doubt His ways. We can rely on Him completely, and therefore on the promises that He makes to us in the scriptures.

Q & A

160. What does it mean to say that God is immutable?

161. Explain how it impacts you personally to know that God never changes.

162. What role could you see this truth playing in an Elder's life as he teaches and counsels hurting or needy people?

Infinite – God is free from all limitations

The scriptures portray and teach that God has no boundaries – in time, space, or being. Let's look at each of those...

Psalm 90:2 says, *"Before the mountains were brought forth, or ever you had formed the earth and the world, from everlasting to everlasting you are God."* Clearly, *time* has no meaning for God – He created it and is outside of it. There is no "before" or "after" for God, there is only what eternally *is*. I've heard this concept described as if all of history were a videotape (*you do remember those, don't you?*). From our human perspective, time passes by one frame at a time. We don't know what's coming next until it actually comes on the "screen" of our personal history. But from God's perspective the entire tape is stretched out beneath Him, and He is able to look down on all of it at once. He is outside of time, ruling over it.

But we also need to realize that God is infinite in terms of *space* – which simply means He is not bound to only one place at a time like created beings. The theological word for this is "omnipresent." God is fully everywhere, all at once. Psalm 139:7-10 makes this very clear, *"Where shall I go from your Spirit? Or where shall I flee from your presence? If I ascend to heaven, you are there! If I make my bed in Sheol, you are there! If I take the wings of the morning and dwell in the uttermost parts of the sea, even there your hand shall lead me, and your right hand shall hold me."*

Finally, we need to try to get our minds around the idea that God is limitless in terms of His *being*. This means that whatever God is, He is perfectly. So, His holiness is ultimate and perfect, as is His love, and His mercy, and His justice, and His compassion, etc. There is no deficiency in God, He is the definition of perfection. Matthew 5:48 says, *" You therefore must be perfect, as your heavenly Father is perfect."* Sound familiar? It should... we've hit this point a few times already in previous sections.

But there's another aspect of God being infinite that we need to consider. It is hard for us to comprehend, but God knows everything. Not only does He know everything, but He knows everything about everything (*1 John 3:20*). That includes everything that is and everything that is possible. This is called God's **omniscience**.

But we must understand that God's knowledge is not obtained by experiencing things or watching events. He possesses all knowledge by virtue of who He is, as God. His knowledge never changes or grows. It is absolute. That means He knows us, our past, our present, our future, and every detail associated with all of those things. There is truly nothing that escapes His notice (*Hebrews 4:13*).

There is a modern-day heresy that is widely accepted in Christian circles today known as "Open Theism" or "Openness Theology." In the Open Theism model, the assertion is made that God knows all things that can be known, which would not include the future, since it does not exist yet.[9] This is where the name of this theology comes from, the idea that the future is "open"

---

[9] See William Hasker, *God, Time, and Knowledge*, (Ithaca: Cornell University Press, 1989)

to God. People who hold this view contend that the future comes into being through the choices of God's creatures who He has given the power of free choice (angels, demons, and people). Once those creatures exercise their power of choice and make a decision, the future becomes present reality. It is only then that there is any reality that God is able to know.

Open Theism is trying to reconcile an apparent tension between the all-knowing sovereignty of God and the seemingly "free" choices of His creatures. However, it is vain attempt that causes many more problems than it solves. First, it makes God subject to time, His own creation, which unravels the very definition of sovereignty (God's rule over all). In Open Theism God doesn't have *total* control. He only has as much control as He is able to have, given the way the system of time operates.

Second, it makes God subject to human whims and decisions. Since He doesn't know what is going to happen in the future, because His creatures haven't yet made choices that determine what that future will be, God is waiting around for us to do something so that He can do something in response. Instead of being omniscient, God is eternally responding.

Third is the issue of predictive prophecy. Given how Open Theism approaches God's knowledge of the future, how do you think it addresses the issue of predictive prophecy? The Open Theistic attempt at reconciling this problem says that since God created man, and time, and has been around for all of history, He knows with a great deal of certainty what will occur, based on that experience. This is how He can accurately predict what is to come.[10] In the final conclusion the God of Open Theism turns out to be a really good guesser, not the sovereign Lord of all.

Fourth, what does an Open Theistic view do to the role of prayer? How can you or I pray confidently to a God who doesn't know what is going to happen, and in some ways is impotent to do anything about our situation until some other being acts? Why would I pray to a God who is not powerful enough to do whatever He wants to do? What assurance do I have that He'll actually be able to do what I ask? Do you see how prayer is emptied of its significance and power? There is no comfort, no real help, and no assurance in prayer in the Open Theism model.

Fifth, and most importantly, the teachings of Open Theism directly contradict the teaching of scripture. For example, consider this passage from Isaiah 41:23, *"Tell us what is to come hereafter, that we may know that you are gods; do good, or do harm, that we may be dismayed and terrified."* God is mocking the idols of Isaiah's day, challenging them to prove that they are indeed gods. He does so by insisting that they tell Him the events of the future, because that is something that only God can do.

In order for the Open Theism model to work, it has to do something with categorical statements like this that are made in the scriptures. There has to be some explanation of why scripture doesn't really mean what scripture says, which can only lead to a diminishing of the authority of scripture. Dr. Wayne Grudem writes, *"Open theism leads naturally to an abandonment of biblical inerrancy, a loss of belief in the trustworthiness of God, and a loss of the gospel itself."*[11] The Open Theistic view of God effectively guts Him of any divinity.

Q & A

---

[10] See John Sanders, *The God who Risks: A Theology of Providence* (Downers Grove, IL: IVP, 1998), p. 131

[11] Wayne Grudem, Contributor, *Beyond the Bounds* (Crossway Books and Bibles, 2003), p. 369

163. Explain what it means when we say that God is infinite.

164. What thoughts go through your mind as you think about God being infinite?

165. How does this reality affect your ability to have faith in God?

166. What does it mean that God is omniscient?

167. How does it impact your faith to know that God knows all?

168. Explain, as briefly as you can, why Open Theism is an unacceptable view of God.

Unity – No division or contradiction within Himself

When we speak of the "unity" of God, we mean that every characteristic or action of God is completely unified with every other characteristic or action of God. There is never a time when there is a conflict within God over what He is, or what He is doing. Again, we've covered this idea a few times already, so I'll not go into great detail. What you need to hear re-emphasized is that God is always in a place of complete harmony within Himself. He doesn't experience the internal conflicts that you and I do. His character is wholly unified in a holy way!

Q & A

169. Is it hard for you to understand the unity of God? Why or why not?

170. How do you see the unified nature of God's character making a difference to your life of faith?

God is Spirit

Jesus tells us in John 4:24 that God is *spirit*. That means He is not composed or made of any material, or energy, or other created thing. God is spirit, a category of being that we struggle to even comprehend. We might think of ghosts or angels or demons when we hear the word "spirit," and in some ways we would not be far off. But what does it really mean when we consider that God is spirit?

At the very least we can say that being spirit means that God is invisible to human sight (*1 Timothy 1:17*), though He has at times appeared to people in forms that they could see (*Exodus 33:21-23*, for example). And – even though God is spirit, He is able to and does reveal Himself to us in various ways (*Hebrews 1:1-3*). He has revealed Himself to us most greatly through the person of Jesus (*Colossians 1:15*). Knowing that God is spirit, we should understand the scriptural references to God that describe Him as having human-like qualities or appearance (i.e., eyes, hands, feet, voice, etc.) are instances of God using human images to help us know about Himself in terms that we can grasp.

Q & A

171. Jesus says that since God is spirit, we must worship Him in spirit and in truth (*John 4:24*). Read that verse and the surrounding context and explain what you think it means to worship God in spirit and in truth.

172. Does the fact of God being spirit make it harder for you to believe in Him or trust Him? Why or why not?

Sovereign – God is in complete control

In human terms we sometimes use the word "sovereign" to refer to a ruler, such as a king or queen. We mean that the person in question is in power or in control over a certain nation. As king or queen, they have the authority to rule. When we use the word "sovereign" in relation to God, we are speaking in the same way but with much greater scope! God is sovereign over everything. Everything. From the atoms in your body to the clockwork precision of the universe, God is in control of everything. Jesus tells us in Matthew 19:26, "*With man this is impossible, but with God all things are possible.*" That means that God has the power to do whatever He determines to do.

Yet, though God is absolutely sovereign, there are some things that He cannot do. What things are those? Things that violate His own character. For example, the writer of Hebrews tells us that it is impossible for God to lie (*Hebrews 6:18*), because of His righteous and holy nature. It is also impossible for God to be tempted by evil (*James 1:13*), for the same reasons. Though it might sound odd to say that a sovereign God has limits in any way, it is these "limitations" that are part of what make Him God! If He were to violate His own character, He would cease to be a holy God. It is probably most accurate to say that God is able to do whatever He determines to do that is consistent with His character.

Q & A

173. Explain in your own words what it means that God is sovereign.

174. Though God is all-powerful, He is not able to do some things. What kind of things can God ***not*** do?

God is perfectly wise

Do you recall the previous teaching about an Elder needing to have wisdom in his leadership? In that section I highlighted an oft-quoted phrase, "Knowledge is knowing the right thing to do, wisdom is doing it." In other words, wisdom is the application of knowledge. In God's case, since He knows everything perfectly, His application of His knowledge is perfect also.

What I'm saying is that God possesses perfect wisdom. He is *able* to do what He *knows* to do in every circumstance, in a way that is *best* and that will bring Him ultimate glory. Said another way, God always chooses the very best outcomes and determines the best ways to get to those outcomes. We see examples of this wisdom in the orderliness and precision of creation (*Jeremiah 10:12-13*) and ultimately in the plan of salvation through Jesus Christ (*Colossians 1:24, Ephesians 3:10*). This truth gives us great assurance when it comes to trusting Him. No matter the circumstance, and no matter the pain or joy it may bring to us, we are able to confidently say that God is doing what is best. That is the message of Romans 8:28, and many other passages in the scriptures. God's wisdom enables us to trust Him more!

Q & A

175.   What does God's wisdom say about His trustworthiness?

176.   Practically, how would this knowledge help you to counsel a person who was struggling with a difficult situation in their life?

177.   How should this truth impact the way you handle worry or anxiety?

God is truthful

Every person we know fails to be completely truthful. Whether a "bald faced" or "white" lie, we are all guilty of lying. Not only that, we also sometimes misrepresent what is true because of our own ignorance. We simply don't know all the facts but speak confidently anyway! Neither of those things ever happen with God. He is absolutely truthful!

Because of His omnipotence, no piece of information ever escapes His knowledge (God is never ignorant). Because of His purity (holiness), God never speaks falsely. Proverbs 30:5 says, "*Every word of God proves true; he is a shield to those who take refuge in him.*" We never have reason to doubt when we trust the Lord. Every prophecy He has spoken will come to pass. Every promise He has made will be fulfilled. We can hold onto God's promises firmly because He will do what He says He will do. We can always know what is true, what is reality, when God has spoken on the subject!

Q & A

178.   Think about the relationships you have in this life. Some are more "trustworthy" than others, aren't they? How is your relationship with God different than that?

179.   How does this truth affect the way you read the Bible?

God is good

We sometimes speak of certain people as being "good." He's a good guy. She has a good heart. But the Bible tells us that in comparison to God, every bit of our human righteousness, no matter how good it may seem, is like a cloth used by a woman during her menstrual cycle (*Isaiah 64:6* – it's what the Hebrew word for "filthy" was commonly used to refer to, really!). Only God

ESSENTIALS FOR THE ELDER: BASIC DOCTRINES

is truly good (*Mark 10:18*).

What this means is that God can only do what is good, what is right – in every circumstance. His is unable to do differently. So, whatever circumstances we see happening, God is in them, working for ultimate good, especially the good of those who are His (*Romans 8:28*). This is very difficult to understand at times, and on a human level may be impossible to completely comprehend. But we can know that whatever circumstances we are facing, God will do what is good and right.

Q & A

180. Imagine a couple losing their baby shortly after its birth. Why would a situation like this make it hard to believe that God is good?

181. What kind of counsel might be helpful to this couple?

182. How does this truth help when you are facing situations where you can't see what God is doing?

God is holy

Many people consider holiness to be equal to perfection. While it is true that God is perfect, that is not what "holiness" means. Literally, holiness refers to something being separated... in this case, it is God being separated from sin. Very simply, holiness means that God is absolutely pure, undefiled in every aspect of His character. One author states that in holiness, God "*eternally wills and maintains His own excellence, abhors sin, and demands purity in His moral creatures.*"[12]

Again, this characteristic applies to every one of God's other attributes. His love is holy. His justice is holy. His mercy is holy. His power is holy. You get the idea? The holy nature of God requires that all of His attributes be the very best that they can possibly be. Spend a little time pondering this characteristic and you'll begin to see that God's holiness makes our redemption all the more amazing.

What I mean is this... we are anything *but* pure, while God is 100% pure. It is His holiness contrasted with our sinfulness that places us under His wrath (*Romans 1:18, Ephesians 2:3*). We are completely outside the realm of what He deems acceptable. Yet, He has provided a way for us to be reconciled to Him through the gift of His Son, Jesus (*1 Thessalonians 1:10, 1 Thessalonians 5:9*). That is truly amazing grace!

Q & A

183. Explain what it means that God is holy.

184. How does it make you feel to know that God expects holiness from you? (*read 1*

---

[12] Lewis Berkhoff, *Systematic Theology* (Wm. B. Eerdmans Publishing Co. / 1996)

Peter 1:16)

185. In view of God's holiness, explain why your salvation is so amazing.

God is righteous

To understand what it means to say that God is "righteous" it is helpful to notice that its root word is "right." To be righteous means that God is, and does what is right, in every case. He judges wrong actions and attitudes justly and is perfectly merciful as needed. He does what is right. We live in a world where justice is not always done. Sometimes, on a human level the guilty go unpunished. But we can confidently rest in the knowledge that God, by virtue of His righteous character, will in every case, put all things right in time. We don't have to fret over what may seem to be His "slowness," or be anxious because of an injustice we have suffered that seems to have gone unpunished. God can be trusted. He knows what He is doing and will carry out what is right in perfect timing.

This brings us to think a bit more carefully about His justice. In our politically correct world, we often get the idea that many kinds of punishment or accountability are mean-spirited, judgmental, or flat-out wrong. Nobody wants to be judged, good or bad. But the truth of the Bible is that mankind is accountable to our Creator-God. He *is* our Judge and will one day call every one of us to account. He has the right to do so by virtue of being the only righteous being that exists. Being perfect, His standard is flawless. Being omniscient, His understanding of every person and every situation is both complete and impartial. He is the only one qualified *to* be judge, and He will judge rightly one day (*Acts 17:31*). There is nothing at all wrong with this... in fact, there is everything right about it!

Q & A

186. Does knowing that God is completely righteous bring any comfort to you? If so, explain.

187. What benefit is there to knowing that every wrong that has ever been done will one day be set right, guaranteed?

188. If we really trust God to judge rightly in the right timing, how will it affect the way we relate to others (those who have hurt us, for example)?

God is glorious

When the Bible speaks of God being glorious, it is referring overall to what God *is* in His essence or nature. His glory is the sum total of everything that He is. So, when God says that He does all things for His glory, He is meaning that everything He does is to point out His glory, His magnificence, the completeness of His nature (*Isaiah 42:8, Isaiah 43:7, Ezekiel 39:21*).

That may sound a bit self-serving or arrogant to you. Just imagine any human being who did everything to draw attention to themselves. You would say they were very self-consumed,

ESSENTIALS FOR THE ELDER: BASIC DOCTRINES

wouldn't you? Why would God do exactly that? It is because the truth is that He *is* perfection, and it is not conceited for Him to believe that and promote it as true. Even more, when God points us to His glory, it is a very loving thing to do, because it is in seeing His glory that we come to desire and trust Him (*2 Corinthians 4:6*). He is perfection, and to see Him for who He is in all His glory, is to see the most desirable and beneficial being that exists!

There is another use of the word "glory" in the Bible. Sometimes it is used to refer to the radiance or light that surrounds God when He makes Himself visible to men (*Exodus 16:10, Exodus 24:16*). We can see this usage of the word most often in the Old Testament, though the New Testament writers do use it on occasion. And, though we don't know for sure *why* this radiant light exudes from God when He does appear, it is clear that there is a meaning behind it. The appearance of light surrounding God is at very least symbolic of the true glory of His nature which we considered in the previous paragraph.

Q & A

189. Explain what it means that God is glorious.

190. Why would God seek His own glory? Is it arrogance? Is it a good thing?

We've tried to highlight some of the attributes of God, but in the end, we will always fall short in our attempts to quantify or describe Him fully. God, in His very being, is truly limitless! Our human minds can only contain so much of the splendor of who He is. But it is in seeking to know Him, that we find our greatest joy!

Jesus: The God-Man

Central to the Christian faith is Jesus – our Savior who we trust and worship as God. In order for our faith, and our confidence in it, to be steadfast, we have to understand how Jesus is both man and God – and why it is important.

Is Jesus really God and man?

It is inconceivable to think that one person could have two natures. It is right up there with the doctrine of the Trinity in terms of difficulty. As theologian J.I. Packer says, "*Here are two mysteries for the price of one – the plurality of persons within the unity of God, and the union of Godhead and manhood in the person of Jesus. Nothing in fiction is so fantastic as is this truth of the Incarnation.*"[13]

i   In the initial years after Jesus ascended into heaven, His dual-nature was one of the first points of Christian doctrine to come under fire. We see in the New Testament itself how the religious leaders of the day could not handle Jesus' claim to be God (*John 8:58-59*). In their minds it was blasphemy for any man to claim to be God... and they were right – but Jesus was

---

[13] J.I. Packer, *Knowing God* (Downers Grove, Illinois: InterVarsity Press, 1993 edition), p. 53.

not *only* a man, He actually *was* God!

The two natures of Jesus

When we speak of Jesus being the God-man, we mean that from the time of His human birth onward, He had and still has two natures; a human nature and a divine nature. Putting the idea of two natures together, we can say that everything that is inherently true of God, is true of Jesus and everything that is inherently true of man, is true of Jesus (except for a sinful nature). And each of these natures is complete. Jesus isn't 50% God and 50% man, He's 100% God and 100% man. Whatever He is in each of these natures, He is fully.

We can see in the scriptures that Jesus is affirmed to have a divine nature. Titus 2:13 says that as Christians we are "*looking for the blessed hope and the appearing of the glory of our great God and Savior, Christ Jesus.*" Do you see it? Jesus is our God *and* Savior! There are numerous times where the biblical writers show Jesus to have the attributes of God. He was omniscient (*Matthew 16:21; Luke 11:17; John 4:29*), omnipresent (*Matthew 18:20, Matthew 28:20, Acts 18:10*), omnipotent (*Matthew 8:26-27, Matthew 28:18, John 11:38-44, Luke 7:14-15, Revelation 1:8*), self-existent (*John 1:4, John 14:6, John 8:58*), and is the Creator (*Colossians 1:16*). We have no choice but to admit that Jesus was and is fully capable of everything that God is.

But why is it important for us to know that Jesus is fully God? What difference does it make? First off, if Jesus had not been fully God, He would not have been able to be perfect in His obedience to God. Why does that matter? Because if He'd not lived a perfect life, His death on the cross in our place would have been no better than yours or mine. As has always been the case, God required a spotless sacrifice to make atonement for our sins (*Ephesians 5:2, Hebrews 10:12, 1 Peter 1:17-19*). Just as importantly, Psalm 49 tells us that no man can ransom the life of another, because the price is too high (*Psalm 49:7-9*). It is vital that Jesus was fully God because only God could accomplish our redemption (*Colossians 1:19-20*).

Q & A

191. List some of the things that the scriptures say of Jesus that show that the biblical writers considered Him to be God.

192. What sort of feelings do you experience as you ponder that Jesus is actually God?

193. Why is it important that Jesus was fully God? What was at stake?

While Jesus has always been God, He has not always been man. His conception in the womb of Mary is the very moment at which He took on His second nature; that of a human. And keep in mind, it's a *second* nature, not another one in place of His first nature. He continued to be fully God as He took on a human nature. If in any way He lost all or even part of His divinity, then He would no longer *be* God.

Why is it important to understand that Jesus was fully human? One of the biggest reasons has to do with His representation of us. It was by one man (Adam) that sin entered the world and brought about death, destruction, and depravity (*Romans 5:18-19*) making mankind guilty before God. The penalty due for sin was directed at humanity, so humanity had to pay the price. In becoming human, Jesus became a legitimate representative for the human race, the one to take the punishment due to every one of us (*1 Timothy 2:5-6, Hebrews 2:14-18*). This issue is so important that John says that anyone who denies that Jesus came in the flesh is of the same spirit as the anti-Christ (*1 John 4:2-3, 2 John 7*). But in being fully God, Jesus was able to be a *perfect* sacrifice, one that would satisfy the justice of God.

Another reason it is valuable for us to know that Jesus was fully human has to do with His role as our mediator and High Priest. The Bible teaches us that though He was tempted in every way that we are, He did not sin (*Hebrews 4:15*). In this way He sympathizes with our human weaknesses completely. When we are tempted, we can be assured that Jesus knows what we are going through by virtue of experience and is able to help us (*Hebrews 2:18*). We have a Savior who can truly identify with us because He is man, and who can also truly help us in temptation because He has never sinned.

Q & A

194. List two reasons it is vital that Jesus was fully human.

195. What difference does it make to you to know that in His time on the earth, Jesus was subjected to every weakness and temptation common to humanity?

Mistakes made about Jesus' nature

From almost the first days of Christianity there has been both confusion and contention about Jesus' nature. Much of the tension happened because the dual-nature of Jesus is very difficult to understand. But it also happened because the scriptures had not been completed or compiled yet, so there was no definite standard by which such matters could be judged.

Theological teachings that are not consistent with what the Bible teaches are called *heresies*. It is important for us to be aware of the various heresies about the nature of Jesus for two reasons. 1) Wrong belief about Jesus will potentially lead to an eternity separated from God. 2) All heresies seem to come back around from time to time. Because of that, it is important for Elders to know why each heresy is incorrect, so that He can shepherd his flock in the truth and guard them from error.

Let's take a few minutes to run through the 6 major errors that have been made regarding the nature of Jesus. Many of them are identified by the name of the person who first taught the heresy, while others are identified by a name taken from a root word having to do with the meaning of the teaching. Just to make it interesting, and to push you to engage your brain, I'm including a Q & A section after each heresy, challenging you to work through *why* each one is damaging to the Christian gospel.

Ebionism: Ebionism is an early heresy stemming from some Jewish Christian circles (*"Ebionite" was the Hebrew term for "poor person"; so, it is supposed that these Jewish*

Christians may have been poor). Since Jews were and are strongly monotheistic (believe in only one God), they denied that Jesus was God, rejected the virgin birth, and believed Jesus was born naturally of a man and woman. In their view, Jesus was human but possessed unusual gifts similar to the prophets of the Old Testament. They believed God's power descended on him in a special way at his baptism.

Q & A

196. While the definition of Ebionism says that this view originated among Jewish Christians, do you think they could truly be Christians given that they held to a view like this? Why or why not?

197. If Ebionism were true and Jesus were just a glorified human being, what impact would that have on our salvation?

Arianism: Arianism is named after Arius of Alexandria, a man whose views were condemned by one of the early church leaders named Athanasius, and by others among the leadership of the church at the Council of Nicaea in AD 325. Arianism also argues for a very inflexible monotheism. Given this foundation, the Arians believed that God alone possesses attributes of deity and to share these with anyone would be to render God less than divine. Therefore, Jesus could *not* have been divine in any way. They believed that "*the Word*" of John chapter 1, was Jesus but means that He was a created being. Some Arians would refer to Jesus as a "demigod," which is an intermediate being, but not God. This is the theology of modern-day Jehovah's Witnesses.

Q & A

198. Does the salvation as we understand it work if Jesus is only a demigod, a non-divine intermediary between God and mankind? Why or why not?

199. Why is this teaching relevant to the day in which we live? Why would an Elder need to be familiar with this teaching?

Docetism: Docetism is based on the Greek word for "seem" or "appear," which hints at its main teaching. In this view it was taught that Jesus only seemed or appeared to be human, but in reality, He only had a divine nature. Part of the reason Docetism came to the forefront was because of the concept of Greek dualism that was prevalent in its day. Dualism teaches that spiritual things are good, but physical or fleshly things are evil. Because of this belief, they could not accept that Jesus had really been a man.

Q & A

200. In this view, which part of Jesus is done away with? Do you understand why they felt this way?

201. What damage occurs to the gospel message if Jesus is not understood to be human?

202. In learning about this heresy, do you learn any lessons about the influence that a culture can have on people's beliefs?

203. How does this cultural impact relate to the role of a modern-day Elder?

Apollinarianism: This heresy comes from the views of Apollinarius. Apollinarius saw Jesus as a compound being: he believed that Jesus was physically human, but psychologically divine. In other words, the divinity that Christ possessed before His human birth is what took the place of His human soul. This view was condemned at the Council of Constantinople in AD 381.

Q & A

204. In this view, how is the truth of Jesus' human nature compromised?

205. What is its effect on the doctrine of salvation?

Nestorianism: This false teaching is named after Nestorius, a church leader in Constantinople in 428. Nestorius had trouble with the idea that the divine and human natures could be united in one person. He felt that to have two natures would obscure both of them. So, he chose to see Jesus' two natures joined in a way which manifested themselves in different ways at different times, off and on throughout Jesus' life.

Q & A

206. What problems do you see with this view? Explain.

207. Is there anything you can see in this view that is similar to modern-day philosophies? If so, what?

Eutychianism: Eutyches was an elderly church leader in the 440s. His motivation in developing his views of Jesus nature was to counter Nestorius's division of Christ which you just read about. The way he did so was by teaching what has been referred to as the "one nature" formula. Eutyches saw Jesus' humanity as completely absorbed into his divinity. A variant of this taught that Jesus' nature was a hybrid of divine and human, and therefore a third, altogether new nature.

Q & A

208. If Jesus' humanity somehow disappeared into His divine nature, what impact does

that have on Him serving as our substitute?

209. If the two natures of Jesus melded together to create a third type of nature, what does that do to the effectiveness of Jesus' substitutionary death?

Should you become an Elder, and perhaps even if you don't, you will find that each of these heresies resurfaces in various forms from time to time. Often "new age" teaching about Jesus is nothing but a rehashed, modernized heresy. If you know these heresies, and where they came from, it will be easier for you to spot them when they crop up. As well, if you think through their errors now, you may not have to refresh too much when you come across them again!

It's important for you to know that one of the main signs of a cult or heretical teaching is that it will deny or attempt to change the nature of Jesus in some way. The problem is this: if you change Jesus, you have changed Christianity! That is why an Elder must be ready to contend for the truth about Jesus... the faith of himself and those he leads depends on the person of Christ!

In addition, knowing the truth about who Jesus is, will greatly affect the way you view Christ and will make the gospel accounts of His life come alive. You will see the amazing God-man, interacting with, loving, and relating to people just like you. And in doing so, you will deepen your devotion to Christ, because as Jesus said, *"If you have seen Me, you have seen the Father"* (*John 14:9*).

WRITTEN QUIZ

In the following questions, do your best to answer without reviewing this section. If you have trouble recalling the information, don't worry – you'll discuss your answers with your mentor!

- As well as you are able, explain what is meant when we say that God is Trinity.

- Does this mean that each of the persons in the Trinity are simply different forms of one God?

- Is each member of the Trinity equal in their divinity? Can you give any scripture to back up your answer?

- Explain why it is important to know that God exists as Trinity.

- List as many of the characteristics or attributes of God as you can remember, with a quick definition of each one.

- Why is it essential that we know that Jesus is both God and man?

ESSENTIALS FOR THE ELDER: BASIC DOCTRINES

- What happens to faith in Christ if we believe He is only divine, or only human?

- What is the word used for a wrong teaching about God?

- Why is it important for an Elder to be aware of various false teachings about God?

> **SCRIPTURE MEMORIZATION**
> *Oh, the depth of the riches and wisdom and knowledge of God! How unsearchable are his judgments and how inscrutable his ways! "For who has known the mind of the Lord, or who has been his counselor?" "Or who has given a gift to him that he might be repaid?" For from him and through him and to him are all things. To him be glory forever. Amen.* - **Romans 11:33-36**

SECTION 7

Essentials For The Elder: Shepherding Yourself

Now that you've learned some of the basic doctrines of the faith, and why the scriptures are such a firm foundation for the Christian life, it's time to put that knowledge into practice. Specifically, let's apply why it is important to know that the Bible is trustworthy, authoritative, inspired, and inerrant. Do you recall Paul's words to Timothy about the profitable nature of the scriptures?

All Scripture is breathed out by God and profitable for teaching, for reproof, for correction, and for training in righteousness. - **2 Timothy 3:16**

If the Bible is the source that every Elder is to use in teaching, reproving, correcting, and training others in the family of Christ, then it is essential that he is allowing the Holy Spirit to do those same things in *his own* heart. A man who attempts to lead others spiritually when he is either unwilling or unable to lead himself spiritually is a hypocrite and should not be an Elder of God's church until that hypocrisy is a thing of the distant past.

This section is aimed at helping you to understand the "how" of Bible study. There are probably as many ways of studying the scriptures as there are people... but there are some "tried and true" methods of Bible study that have proven to be beneficial to a great number of people over the years. In this chapter I will describe and give examples of a variety of ways you can study the scriptures for your own benefit and spiritual health.

Make a plan

Before we get too far into the actual methods of Bible study, something obvious needs to be said. Nothing that we really want to do or need to do happens by accident. You have to do it purposely, intentionally. Studying the Bible is no exception. If you are going to learn and know the scriptures as you should, you will have to *make* it happen. In other words, you need to plan to study the Bible.

To some people planning may sound unspiritual, but it's not. In fact, Paul said that one of the wonderful things the Holy Spirit produces in the life of the believer is "*self-control.*" (*Galatians 5:23*) Why self-control? Because we need it in order to actually do what we *need* to do in growing closer to Jesus! We also need to control self, so that we can do what is needed in order to live as the Lord Jesus desires. Our time studying and applying the scriptures is one of those things that requires the Spirit's fruit of self-control.

The first point I'm making is that you need to **plan a time**. Don't expect that you'll somehow "fit it in" from day to day. You won't. Believe me... you won't. The urgent demands of life will overwhelm your schedule and press out the truly important things like Bible study. In addition, you have a mortal enemy (Satan) who will do everything he can to distract, detract from, and demolish your day so that you will not have time to spend in the scriptures. Beyond all of that, if you are going to be serving your church family as an Elder, you need to be setting the example of what a mature, godly Christian is. Don't give yourself any excuses... you need to plan a time.

And might I suggest you **make it a daily appointment**? If I don't shoot for time in the scriptures *every* day, my week will wind up with more days where I did not study the scriptures than days where I did. Consistency is your ally. Through being consistent you build good habits in action *and* thinking. Your body will even get into the act as you set a regular time for quiet and study. You will become used to that time of study, and you will make good use of it as a result. Don't let your week slip away... make a plan to spend time in the scriptures daily.

I'd also strongly encourage you to **organize your time in the scriptures**. Too often Christians pick up their Bibles without any idea of what they are going to read or study. They resort to an old favorite, or flop open their Bible and read wherever the pages separate. Doesn't the Lord deserve a more diligent effort than that? Don't *you* need something a bit more specific to your life? As a potential shepherd of God's people, you need a plan that guides you through some kind of systematic study, ensuring that you are learning and digesting the entire counsel of God over time.

While there are no magic formulas that will guarantee that you have a great time in the scriptures every day, I'm going to suggest many different methods you can use to head in that direction. But it's up to you to make the time and to organize a plan. And it's up to you to stick with it. A wonderful plan that you don't follow won't do you any good.

Q & A

210. Do you have a scheduled time to study the scriptures? If so, when? If not, what are you going to do about that problem?

211. Do you have a systematic plan for studying the Bible? If not, there are some helpful tools in the following sections.

Roadblocks to your time with the Lord

As mentioned before, we have an enemy who would do almost anything to keep us from finding freedom and power in our study of God's word. Because of that very real fact, we need to be aware of the many types of things he will take advantage of in order to keep us scripturally malnourished. These are the roadblocks to your time with the Lord...

ROADBLOCK #1: No Plan

The previous section beat this drum thoroughly – but I want to pound out that rhythm once more. If you don't have a specific, structured plan for how you are going to go about studying the Bible, it won't happen. It's that simple. If you don't even know how to go about devising such a plan... there are some tools to help you with that in the sections that follow. Once more – make a plan and stick to it!

ROADBLOCK #2: Dependence on Emotions

God's word is truth... it communicates the truth of God. It's important that you have that truth firmly rooted in the depths of your being. Why? Because sometimes what God's word says will line up with how you feel on a given day, but sometimes it won't. When our emotions line up with God's truth, they can be a wonderful blessing. When they don't... we have a battle on our hands. Our task is to base our beliefs solely on the truth of the word of God. Here are some things along these lines for you to think about...

- You know this... but I'm going to say it anyway. You won't wake up each morning enthused and excited about spending time with the Lord. Sometimes the bed will be more inviting, other times you'll be eager to get started with work, jobs around the house... whatever. The point is, you're just not feeling it. Does that mean you shouldn't do it? Giving in to those kinds of feelings/thoughts will be disastrous. The truth is that you *need* that time with the Lord every day. Your day will be worse if you miss it, and your ability to honor the Lord with your life will be compromised – guaranteed. Your desire or lack of desire to consistently carve out that vital time with the Lord has absolutely **nothing** to do with whether or not you should do it. You need it, so do it.
- The time you devote to receiving God's word and praying may sometimes "feel" good while other times it "feels" pretty dry. Does that mean you didn't spend time with God? Does it mean that something is wrong? Does it mean that you aren't "doing it right?" Your emotions are likely to tell you a very loud "**Yes**" to every one of those questions. While there may be some truth there to consider, it's not necessarily true all the time. You need to know that your feelings won't always line up with what is really happening between you and God... and that's O.K. Your diligence and consistency will go a long way to overcome those negative feelings.
- When it comes to the self-discipline needed to stay consistent in your times of connection with the Lord, you cannot allow your feelings to cloud your judgment. When you do... you are being misled to think that you have to "feel" it in order for it to be "real." That's a lie – don't buy it.
- When you do have an emotional experience with the Lord, make sure that you take your

experience to the scriptures for evaluation. Your enemy the devil will be happy to give you all kinds of emotional experiences if they will detract you from living and acting according to God's truth. I'm not saying emotional experiences are bad or wrong – far from it. I'm just cautioning you to keep the truth of God, as revealed in His word, alongside any experiences you may have. Let the word of God interpret, guide, and regulate what you conclude and believe about those kinds of feelings.

- When you have sinned, your feelings will try to convince you that you are "too guilty" to go to God. Are you guilty? *As sin*. But does that mean God doesn't want you to come to Him? Remember David's example in Psalm 51... God will not despise a broken and contrite heart over sin. Go to Him in **spite** of what you feel... in brokenness and repentance. He will receive you, forgive you, and restore you.

Q & A

212. Do any of the scenarios above feel familiar? Explain which ones.

213. Examine your own life for any trace of attitudes that are based more on emotion than truth. Ask the Lord to help you weed those out of your time with Him.

ROADBLOCK #3: Legalism

Legalism is believing that you can actually do something to gain God's favor, when the truth is that you can't. How does legalism become a roadblock to your daily time with God? It hampers the effectiveness of your time with the Lord because you are believing something that is not true. For example: You might be prone to spending a certain amount of time in Bible study, or a certain minimum amount of time in prayer before you "feel right" about making requests of the Lord.

Let's analyze that... you're trying to butter God up with some "good" actions before you ask Him for what is really on your heart. That's legalism, alive and well in your devotional life. God doesn't want your religious actions, He wants your heart... Matthew 15:8 - *"This people honors me with their lips, but their heart is far from me."* It matters more to God that you are honest when you come to Him than whether or not you do all the things you *think* He expects.

Legalism can also make the regularity of your time with the Lord a chore rather than a joy. Anytime your focus becomes centered on the actions you do (consistent time in the word and prayer, for example) and not on the reason behind those actions (because you love God and want more of Him in your life), you can expect your devotion to God to flat-line.

It's that way in all of life. The things you do with great passion are the things you love. When you begin feeling like you have to do them instead of wanting to do them... you are in big trouble. Legalism will kill your love for God. Do your best to keep your mind and heart focused on the greatness of the God you are meeting daily. Remind yourself that the scriptures you will read are *literally* His words to you. Make it personal in an effort to fight of the beast of legalism.

In summary, don't even try to please God. You can't do it. Jesus is the only one who has ever pleased God, and He's the only reason God accepts you. Go to your Father daily in the knowledge of what Jesus has done for you, not because of any kind of righteous things you think you have done. Jesus is your mediator – 1 Timothy 2:5 - *"For there is one God, and there is one mediator between God and men, the man Christ Jesus."* Let what Jesus has done on your behalf motivate you toward humble, grateful love, not legalism.

Q & A

214. Do you think you struggle with legalism? Write down some things you want to watch out for, so that you'll be better aware of how the legalistic trap looks in your life.

215. How does it affect you to think of your time with the Lord as a time of "love, not legalism?"

<u>ROADBLOCK #4: Laziness</u>

You knew this was coming, didn't you? We don't like to face up to it, but it's the sad truth about all of us from time to time. Sometimes we simply don't want to put in the effort it takes to get what we need from our time with the Lord. We want microwave, fast-food spirituality. Add water and stir. But like physical health, a good marriage, competence in your job, and a thousand other things in life that are important, it takes diligent effort to achieve what is needed in your spiritual life. What should you do if laziness is at the root of your problem?

One thing not to do is to allow yourself to begin thinking, *"I've got to get control of this so that God will be happy with me."* That's slipping into that legalistic mindset we just covered. Another dangerous angle of that is this: if you decide you're just going to buckle down and get it fixed, you are likely to slip into an ongoing attitude of self-sufficiency rather than an attitude of ongoing dependence on God as your source of strength. Your best efforts alone won't accomplish what you truly need. So, what *do* you do?

The answer to laziness is self-control. You have to be able to control yourself. But stop a second and realize that true self-control comes from the Spirit of God. Galatians 5:22-23 - *"But the fruit of the Spirit is love, joy, peace, patience, kindness, goodness, faithfulness, gentleness, self-control; against such things there is no law."* If you will turn to the Holy Spirit in an attitude of dependence and *ask* Him to give you self-control, He will give it.

But as a family friends says, *"You can sit naked on the bed all day long and God won't dress you."* Once you've asked the Holy Spirit for self-control, your faith has to go to work! You have to actively *do* what You are asking Him to do in you. If you really believe that He will answer your prayer, then begin doing what the Spirit would have you do as a self-controlled person. You'll find that in the doing, He will provide the self-control you need. Remember, *"as the body apart from the spirit is dead, so also faith apart from works is dead.* - James 2:26.

Q & A

216. Be honest… what ways have you seen laziness damage your regular times with the Lord? Try to be as specific as possible.

217. *"You can sit naked on the bed all day long and God won't dress you."* What things do you need to ask for and begin doing in faith in order to begin having a more committed and consistent time with the Lord?

ROADBLOCK #5: A Wandering Mind

For years I beat myself up over this one. I'd be as little as 5 or 10 minutes into my daily time with the Lord and something completely unrelated would come to mind. Something I had to do at work that day… a conversation I had with my wife the night before… a website I remembered I wanted to check out… the hole in my sock (no joke)… and the list goes on! I'd scold myself for being such a flake, failure, and baby Christian. Somehow, I expected that I should be able to control my thoughts to the point that they would not wander.

You know what I came to realize? Having a distracted mind, though a problem, was not **the** problem. Every one of us has a distracted mind, in everything we do. It's part of being a fallen being. My problem was that I wasn't doing anything to manage that inevitable fact. Then I heard a speaker at a conference address this very issue (I don't recall who it was…). He described my problem in detail and said it was his problem too. But he had found a solution. As you can imagine, I was all ears.

Do you know what his magic solution was? A note pad and a pencil. Seriously. He suggested that when you begin your time with the Lord, make sure you have a note pad and a pencil handy. Then, when the inevitable "to do" task invades your spiritual serenity, you jot it down on your trusty pad with your trusty pencil, so you can get to it later. Then you turn back toward what you were doing with the Lord.

I couldn't believe it could be that simple, but since I decided to try it, it has worked. Don't misunderstand, I still have a wandering mind, but it doesn't have to wander completely away now, because I've learned to off-load those stray thoughts in a way that I'm confident that nothing important will go undone. Give it a try, I'm pretty sure it will be of help to you too!

Q & A

218. Not so much a question as an assignment this time. Get up right now and find a note pad and pen. Put them with your Bible. Use them. End of assignment.

Choosing a Bible study plan

You're now aware of the need to have a plan for your times with the Lord, and I hope you are convinced that it's something you should implement in your life (you are convinced, aren't you?). The question now is, what kind of plan should you use? Truthfully, there is no one answer to that question. And there is no one answer that will be effective for your entire life either. Even the best methods of studying the Bible and praying can become stale over time. It's perfectly acceptable to try out something new from time to time, or to intentionally switch things around to keep it fresh. The unchanging part of your plan is that you choose a time, make sure you have some kind of plan, and stick to it. Exactly what you do when you get there is up to you and God.

But having said that, I'm not going to leave you to re-invent the quiet time wheel all on your own. This section is all about giving you some practical, workable, effective tools for your daily time with the Lord. I'm going to walk through a number of practices that you might find helpful, none of which are original with me, I'm sure. As you read through them, pick out a couple that seem like they fit you, and begin utilizing them in your time with the Lord.

But before we get there, let's consider some basic facts about good Bible study. In order for the scriptures to be beneficial to us, they must be read, understood, and applied. This requires more than simply reading a passage for 5 minutes each day. The kind of benefit we need to derive from the scriptures, and that God intends, can only come as we invest the time to truly *study* the Bible.

When you study the Bible, you are taking time to understand the intricacies of the situations, the logic in the arguments, and the application scripture makes of the truths it is revealing. It may take you a few days to digest one passage or story. It may require that you write the key verses on a card and read and ponder them throughout the day (highly recommended!). All of that is perfectly O.K. Really. You need to get out of the "get er done" mindset. It's not important how fast you finish your scriptural meal, it's important how much nourishment you get from it!

To get started, I'd suggest that you always, *always*, **ALWAYS** begin your study time with prayer. I don't mean that you need to take out your prayer list and pray for everyone from your spouse to your co-worker's Aunt Ethel. I'm talking about an *introductory* prayer, to set the stage and attitude for your spirit and mind. Ask the Lord to help you to understand what He is wanting to say to you through the time you are about to spend in His word. Ask Him to give you an undivided mind, an open heart, and spiritual sensitivity to understand His truth.

The Bible is unlike any other book. You can't simply read it and "get it" immediately. You *need* the Lord to reveal His will and ways to you as you consider the scriptures. His thoughts are much higher than yours, as are His ways (*Isaiah 55:8*). There's no hope of grasping the eternal and unfathomable riches that are recorded in scriptures unless you lean on Him in childlike dependence. *Begin with a prayer of dependence*.

The methods that follow are simply that – methods. None of them are God-ordained or supernaturally inspired, and none of them work effectively all the time, or for every person. They are nothing more than differing approaches to studying the Bible that you may find helpful. You may even find that some are extremely helpful for a season and then lose their effectiveness. Feel free to switch, to try them out, to do what is needed in order for you to stay fresh in your understanding of and desire for the Word of God.

The "S.O.A.P." Method

This method is a "daily devotional" type study method that takes anywhere from 15 to 30 minutes per day, depending on the scripture passage you are using. As far as I know, this method was first devised by Pastor Wayne Cordiero of New Hope Fellowship on the island of Oahu, Hawaii.[14]

BENEFITS
- You can have a meaningful time in the scriptures in a relatively short time.
- Teaches you the basics of how to approach the scriptures wisely.
- Helps you develop the habit of daily scripture study without being overwhelming.

TOOLS YOU'LL NEED
- Trustworthy Bible translation (ESV, LSB, NASB, NKJV, KJV, RSV, NIV)
- A notebook or journal
- A scripture reading plan that covers no more than 1 chapter of the scriptures daily. You can use a ready-made plan or make up your own. You could even begin at the beginning of any Bible book and work through a chapter or less each day, depending on what fits your need.

HOW TO DO IT
- Each day's time in the scriptures will include 4 sections of focus, listed below...

S - *Scripture* – Read the scripture you have chosen for the day. Make sure you take the time to understand what is being said, who is saying it, and why they are saying it. In your notebook, hand write the part of the scripture that stands out to you.

O - *Observation* – Ask the Lord to teach you through the passage. What do you think He is saying to you through what you've read? Paraphrase and write down what you think He is telling you.

A - *Application* – Write out how the passage applies to your life. Are there attitudes or actions you need to change in light of what you've read? Are there conflicts you need

---

[14] http://www.lifejournal.cc/yourdevotions/

ESSENTIALS FOR THE ELDER: SHEPHERDING YOURSELF

to resolve, promises you need to receive, encouragement you need to hear?

P - *Prayer* – Ask the Lord to apply the truths of the passage to your heart. Ask Him for the strength you need to apply what you have learned with honesty.

The S.O.A.P method is a great starter plan, something to get you going in a way that is not too cumbersome or difficult. The only additional suggestion I'd make is that you write down the most meaningful part of the scripture for each day to take with you for review throughout the day (note card, index card, etc.)

Q & A

219. What benefits do you see in the S.O.A.P. Method?

220. How do you think it might benefit your relationship with God?

Scripture/Prayer Method

I'm sure others in the history of the Christian faith have followed a pattern like the one I'm about to teach you, but for me, it's something I sort of discovered as I sought better ways to study and know God's word. I came to this method due to my ongoing struggle to find a practical, helpful way to include study **and** prayer in my daily times with the Lord. My study time was typically good, but my prayer time was typically lacking. I call it the "Scripture/Prayer" method because it centers around meditation on scripture and a prayer response to what you have read and considered. This is one of my favorite ways to spend time with the Lord in the scriptures!

Before I give you a full-blown description of how this plan works, there are two scriptural truths that have helped this method to be of particular value to me:

- God answers our prayers when we ask for things that He wants to give us (*1 John 5:14*).
- Our hearts are sick without Christ. We can't even have the right desires if God does not give them to us (*Jeremiah 17:9, Romans 3:10-18*)

These two, very different scriptural truths combine to help me with this study method in two ways... **1)** As I realize that I am unable to do what scripture is instructing me to do (Jeremiah 17:9, Romans 3:10-18), I find myself more dependent on God and more eager to see Him work in my life to overcome my natural wretchedness. **2)** With that in view, I ask *Him* to do in me what the passages instruct *me* to do... the very things I cannot do on my own. And believing that what He instructs me to be is what He desires me to be, I have great confidence that He will do what I'm asking Him to do, because I'm praying according to His will (*1 John 5:14*)

I can't tell you how much those two truths have encouraged me in my daily walk with the Lord. I'm typically eager, hopeful, and excited to meet with Him because I can't wait to see what wonderful things He desires for me, that I will be able to understand and ask Him for as I meet with Him. And I find myself more eagerly looking for His work being fulfilled in my life, because I *know* He will answer my prayers for these types of things!

After the explanation of this method below, I'll give you an example of it. When you get to the example, notice the underlined verbs in the example prayer...they will give you a better idea of where I put my dependence and hope as I use this method.

BENEFITS
- Will develop a greater appreciation for the heart of what the scriptures are saying.
- Will learn to pray biblical prayers, prayers that ask God for the things He delights to give to His children.
- Will be able to incorporate your personal Bible study and personal prayer together, with some limitations. What I mean by "some limitations" is this: You will be able to study the scriptures and pray during the same daily time. But your "prayer list" will have to be addressed in some other way.
- Can use any passage of the Bible, though the New Testament Epistles and the Psalms and Proverbs lend themselves to this method particularly well.

TOOLS YOU'LL NEED
- A trustworthy Bible translation (ESV, LSB, NASB, NKJV, KJV, RSV, NIV)
- A notebook or journal, or a Bible with wider margins (I first began this method by writing things in my Bible margins but have now decided to use a journal to record more extended thoughts and prayers.)

HOW TO DO IT
- Read the passage you've selected, verse at a time, seeking to understand what the author is saying about God and His relationship with people/the world. Take it in bite-sized pieces.
- Jot down what that section of the passage says about God's attitude toward people, His actions toward them, and what He requires or instructs of the people in question.
- Pray the verse back to God, personalizing as you go (a brief example is below)
- Write out your prayer if that is helpful to you.

EXAMPLE
- **Passage:** Psalm 1:1-2 – *"Blessed is the man who walks not in the counsel of the wicked, nor stands in the way of sinners, nor sits in the seat of scoffers; but his delight is in the law of the Lord, and on His law he meditates day and night."*
- **Notes:** I see that God Himself says that those who have association with people whose lives are characterized by wickedness or sin will not be blessed by Him. He

blesses those who do *not* have those kinds of regular associations. God blesses those who delight in His law, those who meditate on His law consistently.
- *Prayer:* Father, <u>make</u> me to delight in Your word/Your law. <u>Create</u> in me the kind of heart that truly delights in the truths You have to say to me. <u>Make</u> my soul love it, <u>make</u> my mind and heart crave it. <u>Teach</u> me how to seek Your will through Your word. <u>Teach</u> me how to apply it honestly. <u>Give</u> me the self-control and discipline to regularly, habitually meditate on Your word.
- Then move on to the next section of your passage. However, this method is *very* flexible. You can stop mid-way through a chapter if time does not allow you to continue, or you can do more if you are able.

Q & A

221. Do you understand how the scripture and prayer aspects of this method work together? Describe how it might benefit you.

Topical Bible Study

This is a "tried and true" method of learning what the scriptures say about various subjects. Faith, love, hope, joy, the glory of God.... the Bible speaks of all these and thousands more subjects. If you would like an in depth way of studying a specific subject, the topical method is for you. Over time (possibly a very long time), you will gain a comprehensive knowledge of a specific subject.

BENEFITS
- Can truly gain a very comprehensive knowledge of a specific biblical topic.
- Will become familiar with a large portion of scripture, in bite-sized pieces.

TOOLS YOU'LL NEED
- An Exhaustive Concordance for your Bible version *or*
- Decent Bible Software[15]
- A notebook or journal

METHOD
- Choose your topic.
- Look up the topic in your concordance or with Bible software (a concordance in the back of a study Bible will only give you the most important verses where the subject is addressed. To find every instance of a subject, you'll need to use an Exhaustive

---

[15] At www.e-sword.net you can find a down-loadable program that is free, comes with many Bible versions, including the ESV. It's more than adequate for what we are discussing here.

Concordance or Bible software).
- In your Bible, look up the first verse you find about the subject. Read it. Seek to understand the situation and verses surrounding it. Finally, what is being said about your topic? Write down what you discover.
- Move on to the next verse in your list and do the same.
- Continue through the list.
- As you go, you might find it helpful to categorize the ways the topic is spoken of, so that you can keep them separated in your mind.

Please understand, the topical study method is not meant to be completed in one sitting. In fact, it can easily take a good deal of time to complete, depending on what subject you choose and how much time you devote to it in a given day. It's best to view a topical study as a long-term project, one that you will complete by taking baby steps every day.

Q & A

222.   What benefits do you see a topical study having?

Scripture Journaling

This method of Bible study centers around writing down your observations, impressions, and feelings as you read the scriptures. It is similar to both the "S.O.A.P." method and the "Scripture/Prayer" method, but not as structured. One potential drawback to the journaling method (depends on who you are talking to) is that you may become frustrated that you haven't finished with your passage, or even a portion of it by the time your daily time limit is over. But don't let that discourage you from giving it a try. Many people find their study time comes alive as they begin journaling. Dawson Trottman, founder of the Navigators[16] once said, *"Thoughts disentangle themselves as they flow from the lips or the fingertips."* I've found that to be amazingly true in my life. I do at least some journaling as a part of my preparation for almost every sermon, before I turn to any commentaries. It's one of my favorite ways of interacting with the scriptures because it helps me to think through the scriptures for myself.

BENEFITS
- Helps you think through what you are studying with great effectiveness.
- For those who like to write, this method can be a real joy!
- You'll find this method may help you retain more of what you study.

TOOLS NEEDED

---

[16] www.navigators.org

ESSENTIALS FOR THE ELDER: SHEPHERDING YOURSELF

- A Trustworthy Bible translation (ESV, LSB, NASB, NKJV, KJV, RSV, NIV)
- A journal or notebook

HOW TO DO IT
- Choose your passage and begin reading.
- Read enough to understand the context and situation of the passage.
- Hand-write the first bite-sized section of what you've read.
- Begin writing out your thoughts about the passage. Include thoughts, feelings, impressions, questions, life situations it may apply to, examples in your own life that come to mind, other passages that you know relate, etc. There is nothing off limits. In fact, you want to be careful to be entirely honest as you journal about the passage. Write it like a prayer or conversation with the Lord if that is helpful.
- Prayerfully reread what you've written. Add to it if more thoughts come to mind.
- Finish with prayer, asking the Lord to use what you've read to accomplish His work in you.

Q & A

223. What benefits do you see coming from the journaling method of study? Is it something you'd like to try?

The Question Method

This method is actually a part of all the other methods but deserves to be addressed all on its own because of how useful it can be when you focus on it more intently. The question method is exactly what it sounds like. You ask a series of questions about the passage you are considering to help you better understand the context and meaning.

BENEFITS
- This method will open up new doors of understanding for you.
- This method is so easy, anyone can do it.
- This method will force you to look at the context carefully so you can get a more complete understanding of the passage.

WHAT YOU WILL NEED
- A trustworthy Bible translation (ESV, LSB, NASB, NKJV, KJV, RSV, NIV)
- A journal or notebook (optional)

HOW TO DO IT
- Read the passage you've chosen.
- Begin to ask questions about the passage:

- WHO is speaking?
- WHO are they speaking to?
- WHAT are they saying?
- WHY are they saying it?
- WHAT importance does it have?
- WHAT is the main point of what is being said?
- WHEN was this said (in history)?
- WHAT is being said about behaviors, attitudes, or heart motives?
- WHAT does it say to me, my situations, my life?
- WHAT is happening in me as I begin to understand this truth?
- DOES the passage reveal God's thinking or heart about a subject?
- DOES it show me something I should change in my life?
- AND ANY OTHER QUESTIONS THAT COME TO MIND...
- Write down the answers to the questions you ask (optional).

Do you get the point? (Another question there... get it?) These are only suggested questions; you could literally ask thousands of questions about every passage you read. Feel free to make up your own! You'll find that you understand the passage to a much greater degree as you ask and answer questions about it.

The Word Emphasis Method

This isn't really a full-blown study method... it's more of a devotional tool. But it has proven very helpful to me because of the repetitive and varied nature of it. Repetitive *and* varied? Sounds like a contradiction, doesn't it? Keep reading, you'll see what I mean...

BENEFITS
- This method will enable you to hear, read, and speak a particular verse or passage a number of times, which will help to expand the meaning in your mind.
- The repetitive nature of this tool helps you to recall the scriptures you've studied more easily.

WHAT YOU WILL NEED
- A trustworthy Bible translation (ESV, LSB, NASB, NKJV, KJV, RSV, NIV)

HOW TO DO IT
- Take any passage of scripture and read it slowly. A single verse or phrase is usually most manageable.
- Reread the verse, emphasizing the *first* word. Take your time in considering the meaning that emphasis gives to the verse.
- Reread the verse, emphasizing the *second* word. Take your time in considering

the meaning that emphasis gives to the verse.
- Reread the verse, emphasizing the *third* word... etc., etc.

EXAMPLE
- Scripture: John 3:16 – *For God so loved the world that He gave His one and only Son, that whosoever believes in Him should not perish, but have eternal life.*
- *FOR* God so loved the world... (emphasizes God's "reason" for what He did).
- For *GOD* so loved the world... (emphasizes "who" is the primary mover/actor).
- For God *SO* loved the world... (emphasizes the "degree" or "amount" of God's love).
- For God so *LOVED* the world... (emphasizes what God felt/did)
- etc., etc. etc.

Many people find this method to be of great value in getting the full meaning of a particular verse. It can seem somewhat repetitive (really?) but is well worth at least an occasional use.

Q & A

224. How do you see this method being helpful to you? Would you be willing to try it out?

S.P.A.C.E.P.E.T.S. (no, it's not a joke)

This method is another form of the question method, only with more specific questions. The name of this study method comes from an acronym used to help you ask questions of the passage you are studying. I first became aware of this method from Pastor Rick Warren, as covered in his book, "Dynamic Study Methods" which is now out of print.[17]

BENEFITS
- This method will help you to consider the meaning of a passage from a wide variety of angles.

WHAT YOU WILL NEED
- A trustworthy Bible translation (ESV, LSB, NASB, NKJV, KJV, RSV, NIV)

HOW TO DO IT
- Read your selected passage. Perhaps read it again to get a better feel for it. Make sure you have a good grasp of the situation and context, as well as the

---

[17] The closest thing I've found since is, Rick Warren, *Rick Warren's Bible Study Methods*, (Zondervan/HarperCollins Publishers, 2006)

basic ideas.
- Begin walking through the questions below, asking them to yourself as you read the passage again.

In this passage is there any...
- **S**in to confess? Do I need to ask forgiveness of anyone or make any restitution?
- **P**romise to claim? Is it a universal promise? Have I met the condition(s)?
- **A**ttitude to change? Am I willing to work on a negative attitude and begin building toward a positive one?
- **C**ommand to obey? Am I willing to do it no matter how I feel?
- **E**xample to follow? Is it a positive example for me to copy or a negative one to avoid?
- **P**rayer to pray? Is there anything I need to pray back to God?
- **E**rror to avoid? Is there any problem that I should be alert to, or beware of?
- **T**ruth to believe? What new things can I learn about God the Father, Jesus Christ, the Holy Spirit, or the other biblical teachings?
- **S**omething to praise God for? Is there something here I can be thankful for?

Q & A

225. Do you see any value to you in using this type of study? Explain what you mean.

Rewrite/Paraphrase

This method is not an in-depth way to study the scriptures, but a way to help you have a better initial understanding of individual verses or shorter passages. It's not complicated but will take a bit of thought and work on your part!

WHAT YOU WILL NEED
- A trustworthy Bible translation (ESV, LSB, NASB, NKJV, KJV, RSV, NIV)
- A notebook or journal

HOW TO DO IT
- Choose the verse or shorter passage you would like to understand on a deeper level.
- Copy the verse or passage, word for word into your notebook.
- Now re-write the passage in your own words. Paraphrase it.
- Re-read what you've written, comparing it to the original passage.
- If you see anything that you believe you could have/should have done better or differently, re-write the passage again to improve on your version.

ESSENTIALS FOR THE ELDER: SHEPHERDING YOURSELF

Q & A

226. What value do you see in paraphrasing passages of scripture for yourself?

227. Do you see any dangers or things you should be cautious about?

Character Studies

Most of us gravitate toward particular, favorite characters in the pages of the Bible. Jesus, David, Paul, Daniel, Ruth, Mary, Moses... all of these and many more are real people with whom God interacted in a very personal way. Each of them has their own testimony, their own story of what God did in their life. Doing a Character Study is like reading a divinely inspired biography. Through this type of study, you try to get into the sandals of the people of the biblical accounts and learn the lessons they learned, with an aim toward applying their lessons to your life.

WHAT YOU WILL NEED
- A trustworthy Bible translation (ESV, LSB, NASB, NKJV, KJV, RSV, NIV)
- A notebook or journal

HOW TO DO IT
- Choose a person from the Bible whose life story inspires you.
- Find where that person's story begins (a concordance would be helpful).
- Set aside time day after day to read through the various parts of the story of their life.
- Remember to consider things like...
  - The character's background
  - Their occupation or role
  - Their family life
  - The culture they lived in
- Ask yourself...
  - How did God reveal Himself to them?
  - What lessons did they learn?
  - What difficulties did they face and overcome?
  - How did their faith in God enable them to grow and learn?
  - What does their life story teach me about God Himself?

Q & A

228. Write down the study methods that you initially gravitate toward.

229. Another assignment. If you don't have a regular study method that you

use in your daily Bible time, choose one of these methods and begin using it.

The basis of prayer

The scriptures are clear that every follower of Jesus should include prayer as part of their walk with Christ. But did you know that Elders have a special responsibility in this? In the book of Acts, chapter 6 we find a problem that was occurring in the earliest church. Those within the church had spontaneously began sharing each other's needs, financially and in many other ways. In that context there were some widows among them who were not getting enough food each day as it was distributed among the people. The Apostles, the church leaders at that time (and the equivalent to modern-day Elders), were approached with the problem so that a solution could be found. They were the leaders, right? They should take care of this important need, right? They did that, but not by doing it themselves. They appointed others (the first group of Deacons) to take on that task.

Why did they appoint others to take on something this important? Because as the primary leaders of the church, they had some *much more* important things to do. More important than seeing that people who need food are getting it? Yes, *much* more important than that. What were the things they had to do? Read it for yourself, *"Therefore, brothers, pick out from among you seven men of good repute, full of the Spirit and of wisdom, whom we will appoint to this duty. But we will devote ourselves to prayer and to the ministry of the word."* Church leaders are not the ones who are supposed to fix every problem. Don't misunderstand, they are to take the initiative to see that the problems are addressed. But they are not the ones to fix it themselves. They have a higher responsibility that is two-fold: the ministry of the word, and prayer.

A man who desires to be an Elder has to understand this and commit himself to it. The ministry of the word (teaching, preaching, discipleship) and prayer for themselves and the church, are the *main* work of the Elder. Let that sink in. These two are the *main* work of an Elder. The many urgent things that come up week to week in the life of a church are very important. Deaths occur, accidents happen, jobs are lost, sickness comes, spiritual growth initiative and outreach to the community need to be planned and carried out. The Elder is an instrumental part of seeing that all these very legitimate needs are met. But his main *work* is the word and prayer.

Potential Elder, consider that carefully. You are *not* considering being an administrator or organizer, primarily. You are considering being a shepherd of God's people, a spiritual sage and prayer warrior on behalf of your church family. Those are both issues of *work*. As we consider the need for you to shepherd yourself first, prayer is right next to the importance of your time in the word. The Apostles saw these two to be closely linked to each other, and it appears that they thought neither was more important than the other. Do you tend to think of prayer that way? Do you see it as a vital part of your life in and with Jesus?

If you are like most people, prayer is difficult, awkward at times, and truly laborious. In other words, it's not easy to do. Our own sinfulness, the world we live in, our busy lives, and many other things distract us from prayer, and try to convince us that it is not as important as it is made out to be. But the Apostles wouldn't abandon their responsibility to pray even in light of very pressing and life-threatening needs! As an Elder, you need to see prayer that way too. As one author says in the title of his book, as an Elder you are, *Too busy not to pray*.[18]

If you are not a man of regular, diligent prayer, that doesn't mean that you cannot become an Elder. What it means is that you must *become* one. There is no time to lose. Prayer is the source of guidance and insight the Elder needs to do his shepherding task. Prayer is one of the two vital links in the chain of connection to Jesus. Prayer is his line of communication with the Head of the church. Prayer can pull down strongholds and overcome obstacles. Prayer can change lives and situations. Prayer is powerful and effective (*James 5:16*). If you feel the call to be a shepherd of God's people, you must determine, with the help of the Holy Spirit, that you will become a man whose life is characterized, shaped, and defined by the practice of prayer.

Most of us know that prayer is no more complicated than talking... only in this case the one you are speaking to is God. But that doesn't make prayer easy. In fact, prayer can be one of the most difficult and frustrating areas of Christian devotion for many people. This section is designed to help you understand prayer a bit better, and to organize your prayer life so that you can be both consistent and effective at it. Like your time in the scriptures, you will need a plan for your praying, or you won't do it. Same song, second verse!

Before we get to the organizational part, let's consider the foundation upon which prayer is built. Never allow yourself to believe that your right to pray depends on you somehow being worthy of the honor of speaking to God. If that were the case, there is no person living or dead who would ever be worthy of such a wonderful honor! Remember, we're talking about approaching the throne of "*God Most High*" (*Psalm 57:2*)! The only reason we are able to come to the Father in prayer, is because of the life and work of Jesus, our Savior. The Bible tells us that He is our intercessor, making appeals to the Father on our behalf as we pray (*Romans 8:34, Hebrews 7:25*). The instruction to pray "in Jesus' name" (*John 14:13-14, John 16:23-26*) reminds us of that truth.

It's that "in Jesus' name" phrase at the end of our prayers that can often be misleading. Many times, we tack it onto the end of the prayer like some a kind of magical formula we have to say in order to have our prayers received and answered. I've even had people criticize me for failing to say those 3 words in a public prayer before I say, "Amen." That kind of criticism shows me how little people really understand Jesus' meaning when He told us to ask in His name. Jesus was not talking about specific words to be recited when He said that we must ask in His name. What He *did* mean has two different aspects to it.

1) Jesus was saying that when we pray, we should pray for the things that we know will honor Him and the sacrifice that He made for us at the cross. A friend of mine once told me of an illustration his Pastor gave to teach his flock a proper mindset about this issue: He said that it is helpful to imagine prayer as a blank check. To pray in Jesus' name is comparable to filling in

---

[18] Bill Hybels, *Too Busy Not to Pray*, (Inter-varsity Press, 2008)

the amount of the check (your prayer request) confidently expecting that Jesus will be willing to sign the check! "In Jesus' name" is our way of saying, "Jesus, I submit to Your will and Your desires in the situation for which I am praying. I want what You want."

2) Praying "In Jesus' name" is praying with the knowledge that our only access to God through prayer comes through Jesus and what He has done for us on the cross. We are appealing to Jesus' work and sacrifice when we pray "in His name." It's only because of Jesus that we can even speak to God! It is because of Him, and Him alone that the Father should hear us! It is for *His* sake that we ask the Father to give us the things for which we ask! Any answer we receive to the prayer will be for the glory and honor of Jesus. To pray in Jesus' name means that we recognize that we have no right to ask anything of the Father without the merit of Jesus being applied on our behalf.

Q & A

230. Why is it vital that an Elder be a man of prayer?

231. How do you feel about your qualifications in this area of prayer?

232. Would you characterize yourself as a man of prayer, or not?

233. Describe in your own words why we can come to God in prayer at all.

234. Why is it important to keep this in mind when we approach the Lord?

Help in prayer

There are times in life when we desperately need to pray, but due to the agony of soul we are experiencing, or the circumstance that we are in, the words simply don't come to us. The scripture tells us that in instances like this, our prayers are helped by the Spirit of God. Romans 8:26 reads, *"Likewise the Spirit helps us in our weakness. For we do not know what to pray for as we ought, but the Spirit himself intercedes for us with groanings too deep for words. And he who searches hearts knows what is the mind of the Spirit, because the Spirit intercedes for the saints according to the will of God."* In those times when we are too weak to pray with confidence and strength, we have a divine Helper who prays FOR us. The best news about that is that He always prays according to the will of God... so we can expect that His prayers for us will be completely effective!

Q & A

235. What difference does it make to you to know that the Holy Spirit will help you by interceding for you when you don't know what to pray?

Methods of prayer

Throughout the centuries, there have been many "methods" of prayer developed by a variety of people, from ancient Catholic mystics to modern-day writers. While I am unwilling to say that such methods are totally unprofitable, I will say this: the scriptures themselves take a pretty simple approach to prayer. The only model I find is what we commonly call "The Lord's Prayer" or the "Our Father," and even that was given on the heels of a caution that we do not develop formulaic prayers with little personal meaning (*Matthew 5:5-13*). The Bible teaches us that prayer is not a complex thing... it is a humble interaction between the redeemed creature (you) and your Redeemer and Creator (God).

While all this is true, the average person will still find that approaching prayer with some sort of intentional mindset or "structure" can be useful in staying on track and remaining focused on the things that should be prayed about. The Lord's prayer itself shows this to be true by taking the student through a series of "categories" of things to pray about. It models not only content, but also attitude and approach. But keep in mind, the point in developing a structure to help you in your praying is not so that you can say a set of specific words that are somehow more pleasing to God (which don't exist, by the way). The point in using a structure or model is to help you stay focused on the attitudes you need to have while praying and the topics you need to address.

Following are some very basic approaches to prayer, simple tools to enable you to govern your prayer time with some sense of discipline and diligence. As with the Bible study methods, you may find that varying your approach from time to time will help you to stay fresh and maintain your enthusiasm in your prayer times.

Scripture prayer study

This method was covered above in the Bible study section, but definitely qualifies as a method of prayer that is helpful. I have personally benefited a great deal from this approach. However, due to the nature of this method, you will have to make plans to deal with your "list" of prayer requests from friends, family, etc. through some other means.

A.C.T.S.

As long as I've been a believer in Jesus (since I was 5) I have been aware of this acrostic. It centers your prayer time around 4 major areas or types of prayer.

Adoration – In this section you spend time adoring God, praising Him for who He is, what He has done, and what He has promised. Said another way, spend time in personal worship. This element of prayer can really come alive as you spend time in scriptural passages that magnify and extol the virtues and character of God.

Confession – Take time to listen to the Spirit as He brings to mind areas where you have sinned. Humbly and willingly confess those things to God. Confession should be a part of your continual walk with Christ (*Matthew 6:9-13*). Remember that when you honestly confess, God will forgive and cleanse you because of what Jesus has done on your behalf (*1 John 1:9*). Also bear in mind that confession without repentance (a desire to turn from the sin) does little good. It is the one who confesses and forsakes his sin who will receive the Lord's mercy (*Proverbs 28:13*).

Thanksgiving – In our prayers we should always have hearts that are filled with gratitude for all the goodness and blessing our God has poured out on us. We are instructed by the word of God to give thanks as we pray (*Philippians 4:6-7*). This includes thanking God for specific things such as blessings, people, opportunities, guidance, and much more. And don't forget to thank Him for the great gift of salvation that you have received through Jesus.

Supplication – Supplication is an older word, meaning "ask." Under this heading you ask God for the things you need, for His wisdom in the circumstances of your life, for His guidance for you and others. Intercessory prayer (your prayers for others - *Hebrews 10:19-25; Revelation 1:4-6*) fits in here. Spend time praying for specific people, events, government officials, missionaries, the spread of the gospel message, etc. (*Acts 12:5; Romans 10:1*). You may find it helpful to make a prayer list to help you in this section. It is helpful on that list to include a place for answers to your prayers, so that you can use those answers as opportunities for praise and thanksgiving.

Q & A

236.   Can you see this outline being helpful to you in your prayer life? Why or why not?

<u>*Prayer Journals*</u>

A prayer journal is a place where you write out your prayers to God. Think of it has a letter you are writing to God, or a conversation you are having with Him. There are a variety of ways you can organize your journal. Some people purchase a spiral notebook with multiple sections, using those sections to separate different headings or topics of prayer. If you do, you might label the sections as Family, Work, Church, Health Issues, etc., listing your prayer requests in the appropriate section and writing out your prayers as you go. Other people simply begin at the front of their notebook or journal and write out what is on their heart each day in prayers to God (similar to a daily diary, only directed to God).

One of the advantages I've discovered to using a prayer journal is that the process of writing forces me to slow down enough that I'm actually *able* to think through what I really need and want to speak to the Lord about. I find my written prayers are actually more expressive of what is on my heart. A disadvantage, which can become a frustration over time is that prayer journaling requires a decent amount of time. It's simply slower to write out your thoughts than to think them or speak them. Some individuals have tried to overcome that drawback by typing their prayers on word processing or other computer software, and it may work for them. But for me one of the main benefits of journaling is that it *does* take time. I'm forced to think on a deeper level than my hurried life generally allows, and I find myself feeling that I've been able to express my heart to the Lord more completely. There are really no rules for how you journal – you should do what works best for you.

Q & A

237. What benefits do you see to Prayer Journaling?

238. Do you think this is something you will try? Why or why not?

The Lord's Prayer Model

In Matthew 6 we find what we call "The Lord's Prayer" or the "Our Father." Though it was given to us by Jesus, it is not intended to be a word for word prayer that we repeat without meaning. It is to serve us as a pattern or model. Many people find it helpful to follow the outline this prayer follows, similar to how we would follow the A.C.T.S. method. I'll show you how that looks...

Matthew 6:9 - *Pray then like this: "Our Father in heaven, hallowed be your name.*
- Spend time acknowledging God's role as your Father
- Spend time "hallowing" His name... worshiping Him.

Matthew 6:10 - *Your kingdom come, your will be done, on earth as it is in heaven.*
- Acknowledge God's rule over all things in heaven and earth. Submit yourself and your time of prayer to that rule.
- Ask God to bring about His will on earth perfectly, just like it is in heaven. This is prayer that asks God to overcome the consequences of sin in daily, practical matters.
- You could also pray here that the Lord would accomplish His will in the circumstances faced by friends, relatives, etc.

Matthew 6:11 - *Give us this day our daily bread,*
- Similar to the "supplication" part of the A.C.T.S. prayer, this is where you ask God to act on your behalf, to provide, to give you what you need.
- This is another section where you could pray for others and the needs they have.

Matthew 6:12 - *and forgive us our debts, as we also have forgiven our debtors.*
- This is where you would confess your sins and failings.
- Ask the Lord to forgive you because of Jesus' death on your behalf. Ask Him to give you the strength and ability to turn from that sin consistently.
- Ask the Lord to show you any situations where you need to offer or give forgiveness to someone else or pursue reconciliation with another person.

Matthew 6:13 - *And lead us not into temptation but deliver us from evil.*
- Ask the Lord for protection from temptation, Satan, sin, and your own selfish inclinations.
- Ask the Lord to make you strong in your faith when these temptations do come your way, so that you can honor Him in that moment.

This example is just a rough outline. Feel free to fill it in with more details of your own.

Q & A

241. What benefits do you see to following the Lord's Prayer as an outline for your prayer life?

I. O. U. S.

I first heard of this method in a series of lectures given by Pastor John Piper on the topic "Fight for Joy." Since that time, I have discovered that he covers this method of prayer in one of his books.[19] The idea is very simple: Find scriptures that request the Lord's help in a personal way and pray them back to God for yourself. Piper says that he uses this method himself, almost every day of his life. I can see why... it is very helpful in at least two ways. 1) It points out your own weakness and your need for the Lord. 2) It directs your soul toward the things that God desires for you. The letters in the acronym stand for the first word in 4 different passages from the Psalms. If you will take the time right now to look up these 4 examples, you will notice that the verses surrounding them lend themselves to this kind of use as well. Here's the outline of I.O.U.S....

I. - *Incline* – Psalm 119:36 - *"Incline my heart to your testimonies, and not to selfish gain!"* Use this example from the life of David to ask God for the inclination to desire His word. He delights to answer this kind of prayer!

O. - *Open* – Psalm 119:18 - *"Open my eyes, that I may behold wondrous things out of your*

---

[19] John Piper, *When I Don't Desire God*, (Desiring God Foundation, Published by Crossway Books, 2004)

law." Ask the Lord to open your eyes, that you can see the amazing truths that lay within the pages of His word.

U. *- Unite* – Psalm 86:11b - *"unite my heart to fear your name."* We must face the reality that we have divided hearts. We rush after too many things, forgetting that what we really need is a heart that is united in pursuit of God. Ask the Lord to unite your heart to fear Him.

S. *- Satisfy* – Psalm 90:14 - *"Satisfy us in the morning with your steadfast love, that we may rejoice and be glad all our days."* Ask the Lord to satisfy you with Himself, with His love, with the things of God.

Q & A

242. What benefits do you see coming from this method of prayer?

243. How important do you think it is for scripture to inform the way you pray?

244. How does this method help in that?

The Prayers of Paul

You may have noticed that in almost all of his letters to the churches, the Apostle Paul records some kind of prayer that he has been praying for those to whom he is writing. I'm so glad that the Holy Spirit had him do that, because those prayers have been of tremendous help to me in learning exactly *what* kinds of things I should be praying about. I tend to get stuck in certain types of prayers… "Lord, be with him…," "Give her strength…," "Help him…" Please understand that those types of prayers are fine – for as far as they go. But honestly, they don't go very deeply into the areas of life and heart that truly matter. Paul's prayers give us a great example of what these "deeper" kinds of prayers may look like.

You can find the prayers of Paul in almost all of his letters. Some of my favorites are found in Ephesians 1:15-23, Ephesians 3:14-19, and Philippians 1:9-11. For sake of illustration, let's take one of those and walk through it so that I can show you how I personally benefit from using Paul's prayers as models after which I can base my own prayers.

> *And it is my prayer that your love may abound more and more, with knowledge and all discernment, so that you may approve what is excellent, and so be pure and blameless for the day of Christ, filled with the fruit of righteousness that comes through Jesus Christ, to the glory and praise of God. -* **Philippians 1:9-11**

Do you see the kinds of things that Paul thought important to pray about? He prayed that these Philippian believers would be given the knowledge and discernment they needed, *so that* they could know and approve what is excellent (by God's definition)m, *so that* they could be pure and blameless when Christ returned, filled with the fruit that a righteous life produces. And he prayed all of this so that their lives would give glory and praise to God!

Paul prayed for people according to what I call an "eternal perspective." He looked beyond the current circumstance, though it may be very oppressive or dangerous, and looked to the end goals that Christ had for the people in mind. He looked at their situation and analyzed what they truly needed in order to grow into a mature faith, and asked God *specifically* for those things. These kinds of prayers are much more than, "be with them..." kinds of prayers! These are prayers that seek the power and wisdom of God on behalf of others, in specific and intentional ways.

Take some time right now to skim through Paul's letters and find some other examples of this type of prayer. Pay attention to the types of things Paul asks the Lord to do for others. If you are anything like me, you will begin to see that the kinds of prayers you have been used to praying are somewhat anemic by comparison. If you'd like to explore this idea a bit more thoroughly, Dr. D.A. Carson has written a very helpful and excellent book on exactly this subject![20]

Q & A

245.   Find one of Paul's prayers right now. Spend some time thinking about the "kinds" of things he prays about. Write them down in some general categories.

246.   Compare the typical prayers you pray to the type of prayers Paul prayed. Honestly, what is the comparison?

247.   Do you see any ways that Paul's example can be helpful to you?

Help from the Psalms

A final way to approach my praying that has benefited me since my college days, when I first became aware of it, is to look to the Psalms as examples of how to pray. In the songs of Israel's spiritual leaders, we find a wide variety of prayers, both in type and in approach. There are laments, complaints, requests, praises, thanksgivings, and many more. There are even prayers asking God to destroy enemies (in not so pleasant terms sometimes).

The main benefit the Psalms have added to my prayer life is that they demonstrate for me that there are not any "inappropriate" types of prayers. I can cry out to God. I can ask for justice. I can express anger, or disappointment, or frustration to Him. I can complain if I feel that I'm being treated unjustly in some way. But I don't stop there, because the Psalms have

---

[20]D.A. Carson, *A Call to Spiritual Reformation: Priorities from Paul and His Prayers* (Baker, 1992)

another, equally important lesson for me... that no matter what I express to God in prayer or how I express it, I am to eventually come to the place that I submit to His will in everything. In short, I am to fear Him, even in my times of frustration and complaint.

Look through the Psalms right now. Notice the different types of prayers that are contained in them. But also notice that in almost every Psalm that is of a "negative" tone (complaint, asking for vengeance, etc.), they end with praise to God for being God. There is an ongoing theme of humble submission throughout the Psalms. We would do very well to learn both how to be completely open and honest with God, and how to fear Him appropriately in our honesty.

Q & A

248. Do you ever feel stifled in your prayers because you are afraid to be honest? Does it seem like the writers of the Psalms felt that way?

249. Do you understand that God is able to hear what you have to say, honestly, from the heart?

250. Explain in your own words what is meant by "fearing Him appropriately in our honesty."

Organizing your prayer priorities

For years, I struggled to find a way to include the many things I needed to pray for and about, into a system of some kind so that I wouldn't overlook or forget them. I wanted to be diligent in my prayers for my family, friends, and church family, but felt that the great number of things I should be praying for was so overwhelming that I couldn't get through it! I thought that I'd never be able to consistently pray for all those needs! I tried to write out my requests on a "list" so that I could systematically go through them. But I found that the truly important things were placed on the same level as the "not so important" things, which kept me for praying for the more important things as often as I felt I should. I also found that the list kept growing and became unmanageable over time.

One year when I was attending a conference, I heard Dr. D.A. Carson (author, and professor at Trinity Theological Seminary) speaking. In his message, he made a side comment about the way he went about organizing his prayer life. He had a very simple, easy-to-follow system that enabled him to regularly and consistently cycle through all of his prayer concerns. He had my attention! I began using his system and found it very helpful. Over the years I have adapted it in a few significant ways. It has been a wondrous blessing to me. It's no cure-all but is a very practical way to organize your many prayer requests into a system that works. I call it *the 3 stack method* – and here's what I do initially to get it organized...

- STEP 1: I write a list of everything and everyone that I want to pray for on a regular basis.
    - This is everything from my wife and children, to individuals in my church family, to ongoing personal needs, to my country and its leaders.
    - This helps me to have a pretty full idea of the things I want to be praying for.
- STEP 2: I decide *how often* I want to and need to pray for each of those individual prayer concerns.
    - Some people or things, like my wife and children, I want to pray for daily.
    - Others, like specific families in my church, or temporary situations, I don't feel a need to pray for as regularly – though I do want to be faithful to pray for them consistently.
    - Finally, there are issues or needs that are even lower on the priority scale than that. It's not that these are unimportant or shouldn't be prayed for, but that they are not AS important as some of the other things on my list.
    - I assign one of 3 priorities to each of them. I've decided to call those 3 levels of priority "Daily", "Weekly", and "Rotation" requests.
- STEP 3: On index cards or note cards of some kind, I write each request, one to a card (you'll understand why in a minute).
    - Somewhere on the card, in large letters, I write it's priority, so that if they accidentally get mixed up, I can re-sort them easily.
    - Then I place each card in a stack with the other cards of the same priority.
    - Here are some examples of how my cards look...

- STEP 4: Using paper clips, I group each stack so they don't go flying across the room if I drop them! So now I have 3 stacks of requests, each with a different priority assigned to them.

- HOW IT WORKS: Here's where it gets really practical... and where you will begin to understand why I'm using paper clips!
    - Every day when it comes time for me to pray, I take the "daily" stack, remove the paper clip, and pray for each request in that stack, from front to back. When I finish

ESSENTIALS FOR THE ELDER: SHEPHERDING YOURSELF

  - praying for a request, it moves to the back of the stack. When I finish praying for the next one, it goes to the back of the stack, and so forth until the entire stack is finished. Then I reattach the paper clip.
  - When I'm finished with the "daily" stack, I move on to the "weekly" stack and pray for an equal amount each day. (For example: If I have 21 cards in my weekly group, and if I have my prayer time 7 days a week, I'll be praying for 3 per day. Again, as I finish each request, it goes to the back of the stack. When I'm finished with the assigned number of cards in the "weekly" stack, I reattach the paper clip. Since I moved the requests I prayed for today to the back of the stack, the first one on the stack will be where I start the next day.
  - When I'm finished with the "weekly" stack, I'll move on to the "rotation" stack. I don't have a specified number that I pray for in this stack, just whatever I have time for. Again, as I finish each request, it goes to the back of the stack. When I'm finished, I reattach the paper clip to the stack of cards.
  - What happens if I run out of time or an emergency comes up? Even if I didn't finish one of the stacks as planned, I just paper clip it where I left off, and pick up there the next day, resuming my normal routine. I never worry about "catching-up" if I have fallen behind for some reason. I just pick up where I left off.
  - You should keep your 3 stacks in something where they won't get lost or misplaced. You could use anything from a zip-lock bag to a file folder, to a briefcase pocket. I have a zippered pocket folder where I keep mine. Just make sure you keep it in the same place all the time so that when it comes time for you to pray, you know where it is!

- ADDING/REMOVING ITEMS
  - Any time a request is no longer relevant, you can simply remove that card from the stack and throw it away.
  - For answered prayers - you could create a 4th stack of "Answered" requests that you could periodically look through in order to give additional praise to God for His answers! You could even place a single card in any of your other stacks that says, "Praise for answered prayer." When you get to that card, take out your 4th stack and praise God for some of those things!
  - If the priority of one of you prayer items changes for some reason, you can reassign it to another category by making a new card for it.
  - The most difficult part of this system is in handling new requests. If someone asks you to pray for them, you first have to remember to write down their request, so you don't forget. I often take out my cell phone on the spot and send an email to myself reminding me to add that request to my stacks (I tell the person what I'm doing so they don't think me extremely rude!). Once that is done, all you have to do is to make a card for their request, assign it a priority, and include it in the cards you

already have in that stack.
- Sometimes you might be given a prayer card from a missionary family, or another ministry that contains its own list of specific requests. Or you might be part of a prayer chain or other distribution list where you receive lists of requests on a regular basis. You can make individual cards for every individual request if you'd like, but I don't go to that trouble. I include those kinds of cards or lists in my "rotation" stack. When I get to that card, I pray for as many of the individual requests on it as I can. If I don't get all the way through, I leave it on the front of the stack and mark with a pencil next to the request where I should begin praying next time.

I've found this method to be a great help to me in organizing the many things that I need to pray for. It allows me to truly be regular and consistent in praying for the things that are important to me, or that are my responsibility to pray for as a father, husband, Pastor, etc. Now, I can honestly say that I've been praying for people on a regular basis – and encourage them by telling them so!

Q & A

251. Are you well enough organized in your prayer life?

252. Do you think this method could help you in that?

253. Why is it so vital that church leaders have these kinds of personal habits well-in-hand?

ESSENTIALS FOR THE ELDER: SHEPHERDING YOURSELF

WRITTEN QUIZ

In the following questions, do your best to answer without reviewing this section. If you have trouble recalling the information, don't worry – you'll discuss your answers with your mentor!

- Explain what is meant by the term "shepherding yourself."

- Why is it vital that Elders are in the habit of doing this?

- What benefits come from it for the Elder? For the church?

- What role does Bible study have in this?

- How often should an Elder to be studying the word of God? Why?

- Explain why it is important for Christians to have a planned time and way in which they are going to study the word each day.

- What role does prayer play in this task of shepherding yourself?

- What are the two specific things said to be an Elder's responsibility? (HINT: Acts 6:4)

- What benefit does prayer have for the life of the Elder? For the church he leads?

- Explain why it might be a good idea for an Elder to have some kind of system to organize his prayer life.

> **SCRIPTURE MEMORIZATION**
> *For the word of God is living and active, sharper than any two-edged sword, piercing to the division of soul and of spirit, of joints and of marrow, and discerning the thoughts and intentions of the heart.*
> **Hebrews 4:12**

SECTION 8

Essentials For The Elder: Communicating The Gospel

I've intentionally left this chapter to the very end of the training handbook for one very simple reason. I want it to be echoing in your mind as you finish this course. Why? Honestly, there are multiple reasons why I want it to be the last thing you consider. Partly, it's because of what's happened in my own life in regard to the gospel message. I became a believer at the wise old age of 5, and realize now that though my conversion was genuine, there was much about the gospel that I did not understand. Though I've experienced much of church life, in a variety of differing church traditions, I've come to see that there are many views on the gospel within the church, and not all of them are helpful, and some of them are not even biblical.

For example, I've received training (formal and experiential) in contexts that promoted a "Lordship" type salvation message (meaning that you accept Jesus as Lord at the same time you accept Him as Savior… or else you haven't really accepted Him at all), and in churches that were very combative toward that kind of approach, insisting that anyone who calls on the Lord in faith, regardless of any subsequent fruit or lack of it, has full assurance that they are eternally saved, regardless. I've heard the arguments on both sides and have actually made some of those arguments myself over the years.

If I've come to know anything about this subject, it is this: the gospel message matters… a lot! I say that because what *makes* us Christians is the good news of the gospel of Jesus Christ. The gospel is what makes the first and primary difference in the life of any person, and it is the *only* "change agent" the church *has* to apply to the lives of unsaved people. As Paul said, it is *the gospel* that is the power of God, for the salvation of everyone who believes (*Romans 1:16*). What is more, it is a deepening understanding and grasp of the gospel that reveals the everlasting wonders of the grace, mercy, and love of God which cause us to grow into maturity in Christ.

If we miss this, we miss everything. If we get the gospel message wrong, we have Christianity wrong. It is vitally important that we do the necessary work to both understand the gospel and to communicate it completely, with clarity. If we don't, we could be mishandling or mistakenly abbreviating the most important news ever to be proclaimed on this planet! So, in this last section we are going to make sure that you are clear on the gospel. What does *not* qualify as the gospel, what *does* qualify as the gospel message, and how do we *communicate it* to others effectively?

Q & A

254. Why is it important that you clearly understand what the gospel message is?

255. How do you see this relating to your potential role as an Elder? In other words, why is it important that *Elders*, have the gospel straight?

256. As a "before and after" exercise, briefly write down what you consider to be the main points of the gospel message. You'll be given the opportunity to check your response with the actual gospel later on.

Not the gospel

There are many things being referred to as the "gospel message" in our day that fall miserably short of the whole truth. For example, many will say that loving people in practical ways is one way that we share the gospel. From food kitchens to homeless shelters to medical clinics in the jungles of Peru, Christian ministry to the *"least of these"* (Matthew 25:40, 45) is seen as an effective way of sharing the gospel message. But does the scripture bear this out? Look at what Paul says...

> *For "everyone who calls on the name of the Lord will be saved." How then will they call on him in whom they have not believed? And how are they to believe in him of whom they have never heard? And how are they to hear without someone preaching? And how are they to preach unless they are sent? As it is written, "How beautiful are the feet of those who preach the good news!"... So faith comes from hearing, and hearing through the word of Christ.* - **Romans 10:13-15, 17**

Notice the points Paul makes.

1. In order for people to be saved, they must "*call on the name of the Lord.*"
2. They can't call on the name of the Lord if they don't believe in Him.
3. They can't believe in Him if they never *hear* of Him.
4. They will not hear of Him if nobody *tells them* about Him.
5. Faith comes from *hearing*, and hearing comes through the word of Christ.

To put it in a nutshell, the gospel is a verbal message (spoken or written) that teaches people about their own need to call on the name of the Lord so that they can believe in Him. It is a proclamation of truth about the way to be saved from sin. Compassion ministries of various kinds can be very helpful in gaining a hearing or showing the love of Jesus through such service, but if it is not accompanied by a clear, verbal presentation of the facts concerning God's way of salvation as revealed in the word of God, then the gospel has not been shared. As someone once said to me, *"You may have filled their bellies, but were they to die later that day, they'd still go to hell, only on a full stomach."*

We must understand that as helpful and appealing as practical, need-based ministries are, they do not change the heart of one person. Paul says that it is the gospel that is "*the power of God for salvation, to everyone who believes*" (Romans 1:16). Did you catch that? *The gospel message itself* is the power of God to save people. So, in one sense, it doesn't really matter how slick or appealing our "programs" are in drawing people in and softening up their resistance to hearing about Jesus. If the gospel message is not clearly communicated, they will not be saved. Period.

In the church that I am blessed to help lead, we make a point to include the gospel message, in some form, in every ministry endeavor. One example is that we partner with a low-cost food program to help those in our community who are in need. We offer this ministry as a church for many reasons: Among them are these two: so that we as a church can genuinely love others in Jesus' name, to open doors into people's lives with the hope that we will be able to build a relationship. But why are we wanting to build that relationship? Because our love for them compels us to share the good news of Jesus Christ with them. We know that we may not get the opportunity to do this in a spoken form with every person, so we are happy that the organization we work with includes a clear gospel plan in every food box that goes out.[21]

The gospel message is a *verbal* message. It is communication of God's truth to someone who has not embraced that truth. That doesn't happen through kindness or loving actions alone, words must be spoken if it is going to happen.

Q & A

257. Does *sharing the love of Jesus* in a "need meeting" setting seem to be a sufficient way to share the gospel?

258. Explain why such ministries are good, but not enough.

What IS the gospel message?

Now that we're clear that the gospel is a verbal message, we should pin down what that message specifically is. The word "gospel" actually means, "good news," which it surely is. But what good news are we specifically talking about when we say "the gospel?" It is the good news concerning Jesus Christ. Surely there are many ways to outline or communicate the main points in the gospel message, but the following outline, borrowed from Will Metzger's wonderful book[22], is the most helpful that I have found. It is clear, easily communicated,

---

[21] See www.angelfoodminstries.com
[22] Entire outline is based on, Will Metzger, *Tell The Truth: The Whole gospel to the Whole Person, by Whole People*, (Intervarsity Press, 2002), Appendix B

simple, and biblical. There are 4 basic points with some teaching to go under each of them.
God – Man – Jesus - Response

God – SCRIPTURE: *Acts 17:22-34*

It's vitally important that we begin any presentation of the gospel with a clear definition of God Himself. The reason should be obvious, but let me state it anyway. When people today say, "God," they don't all mean the same thing, do they? Some may think of the pantheistic concept of God we spoke of in the section on the Trinity. Others may think of some type of "goddess" or pagan god. Others may think of a "higher consciousness" of some kind. It is **vital** that we start any conversation about the gospel with a biblical definition of God. Without it, we have no hope of getting across the essentials of the gospel message. That is because it is the *just* God of the Bible who has been offended by our sin, and it is only the *merciful and all-powerful* God of the Bible who can save us from our sin. If they don't understand who God is, they won't understand their offense, or God's desire and ability to save them. In short, if they don't see God for who He really is, they won't see *why* the gospel is necessary.

So, what specifically needs to be taught about God? We've already considered a ton of things about God in this handbook. Do all of those things need to be told to every person who is listening to a gospel presentation? No, there are really only three main things they need to know about God in order to understand the need for the gospel: God is #1 our *Creator*, #2 our *Father*, and #3 our *Judge*. Let's consider each, briefly. It will prove helpful if you open your Bible to the passage listed at the top of this point so you can see how Paul makes these points in his conversation with the Athenians.

- *Creator* – As your Creator, God owns you and created you for His purposes. He has the right to your life. Therefore, you are accountable to Him, at the very core of your being.
- *Father* – Besides being your Creator, God loves you, as a Father. Because He loves you like this, He desires you to be "at home" with Him, as His adopted spiritual child.
- *Judge* – In love, God has given you His law (the Bible) to show you the right way to live. Since He is the law-maker, He is also your morally perfect Judge, whose laws are to be obeyed.
- Summary Point: Since God made you, you belong to Him and are accountable to follow His instructions for a relationship of love centered on Him.

Q & A

259.   Look at Acts 17:22-34. How does Paul make the point that God is our Creator?

260.   Given the setting (Paul being in Athens), explain how Paul is attempting to educate these men about the *true* nature of God.

ESSENTIALS FOR THE ELDER: COMMUNICATING THE GOSPEL

261. What does Paul say to show the Athenians that God is loving?

262. What does Paul say to communicate that God is our Judge?

263. In your thinking, why do people need to know these things in order for the gospel message to make sense?

Man – SCRIPTURE: *Romans 3:23, Romans 6:23*

Next, we need to make sure that we communicate the truth about mankind. If we don't clarify why we need to call on the name of the Lord, people won't see a reason to do so. For example: Next time you see a commercial, watch it closely. In most cases, the advertising agencies have learned that if they don't start out by showing you why you "need" their product, they will have a very hard time convincing you to buy it. But if they can make you believe that you can't live without their product, you'll have no problem buying it. That's what the "Man" section is about. You aren't "selling" the gospel, but you are showing people their *need* for the gospel. In this section there are 3 points here as well: #1 We've failed to obey and love God, #2 our sin separates us from God, #3 sin is punished by a God of justice. Let's take one at a time. Again, open your Bible to the passages listed above to see how Paul makes these points.

- ***We've failed to obey and love God*** – Anyone who fails to live by God's rules for life has disobeyed the God who made the rules. The Bible calls this sin.
- ***Sin separates you from God*** – Your relationship with God is now broken. There is a huge gap and you are unable to please God and change for the better.
- ***Sin is punished by a God of justice*** – God cannot overlook sin; He must judge and punish those who sin and have turned from their loving Father.
- <u>Summary Point</u>: Having become self-centered, you are separated from God, unable to earn forgiveness, enslaved to your desires, experiencing guilt, and headed down the road to a hopeless eternity.

Q & A

264. Look at Romans 3:23, and Romans 6:23. In these verses, how do we see the points made in this section – We've failed to obey and love God, Sin separates you from God, and Sin is punished by a God of justice?

265. In communicating the gospel, why do you think it is important for a person to understand their own guilt before God?

266. Why is it important for people to see that they can do nothing to earn God's

forgiveness or make up for their sin?

Jesus – SCRIPTURE: *Romans 5:6-10*

This section provides the solution for the need you just raised. It holds up Jesus as God's only avenue of escape from His righteous judgment. Let's look at the main points: #1, God provided a bridge back to Him through Jesus, #2, Jesus became our substitute, #3, Jesus rose from the dead. Please, look over the passage above as you consider these points.

- *God provided a bridge back to Him through Jesus* – God came as a man, in the person of Jesus because He loves you.
- *Jesus becomes your substitute* – Jesus became our substitute by perfectly obeying all God's requirements on our behalf, and by taking the punishment due because of our sin when He died on the cross. This frees us from our enslavement to sin and satisfies God's just judgment of our sin.
- *Jesus rose from the dead* – Jesus defeated death by coming back to life. God the Father accepts Jesus' substitution for us and offers us true righteousness and forgiveness because of Jesus' victory over sin and death.
- Summary Point: God initiated a solution to our problem by offering His Son Jesus. This provides us the free gift of forgiveness and righteousness, which bridges the gap between us and God. Instead of trying to earn our own righteousness (which we could never accomplish), Jesus gives us His perfect goodness.

Q & A

267. Look at Romans 5:6-10. In these verses, how do we see the points made in this section – God provided a bridge, Jesus becomes your substitute, and Jesus rose from the dead?

268. Why is Jesus the only adequate substitute for us?

269. Why is it important for a person to see Jesus as their substitute before God?

You might say the first two points – God, Man – were the "bad news." This point, "Jesus" is where the good news begins. But we're not quite finished. Though the good news has been revealed, it has to be accepted by each person, and that comes in the final point, "Response." Again, there are three points: #1, God, your Maker, calls you back to Him, #2, Turn, and #3, Trust. Read the passage listed below to see how it fits into this point.

Response – SCRIPTURE: *Romans 10:9-10*

- ***God, your Maker, calls you back to Him.*** - You are to do more than just intellectually acknowledge these historical facts, you are to wholeheartedly respond to the force of these truths in two ways.
- ***Turn*** – This is called "repentance." You choose to turn from your sinful lifestyle and efforts at self-justification and surrender to God's ownership of your life.
- ***Trust*** – This is called "faith" or "belief." You are to trust in Jesus, the one who obeyed the Father perfectly and died in your place. In trusting Jesus, He will enable you to follow God's plan for your life.
- <u>Summary Point:</u> God has done all this for you because He made you and loves you. How will you respond?

Q & A

270. Look at Romans 10:9-10. In these verses, how do we see the points made in this section – God calls you back to Him, turn, and trust?

271. Why is it important for a person hearing the gospel to understand that faith is more than intellectually agreeing with the facts about Jesus?

272. Explain what it means to "trust" in Jesus for forgiveness and new life. How is this different from "turning over a new leaf?"

Clearly communicating the gospel message

As you can see, there are some very specific and basic truths that are to be included in any gospel presentation. Without knowledge of God as Creator, Father, and Judge, a person has no *basis* upon which to understand their need. Without a realization of their own rebellion against that God, they have no *reason* to consider that they might need forgiveness or new life. Without an understanding of what Jesus has done, they will have no *way* to move from condemnation to forgiveness, and without a response, they will not *receive* any of the blessing or transformation found only in Jesus.

In order for you to be able to clearly and fully communicate the gospel message, I encourage you to learn the 4 headings presented above, along with the scriptures and points under each one. Write it out on a card, review it as you drive, or take your lunch break. Practice saying it aloud and learn it as you would learn a set of details you would need for a project at work. You need to have this information readily available, at a moment's notice. Should you become an Elder you will need to have a complete and clear way to explain the gospel message to people.

Review it not only so that you can share it easily with others when the time comes, but also so that your own walk with Christ will be enriched. Every lesson we learn in the Christian life flows out of the basic facts of the gospel. Jesus is the center, and His life, death, and resurrection are central to living as God would have you live.

WRITTEN QUIZ

In the following questions, do your best to answer without reviewing this section. If you have trouble recalling the information, don't worry – you'll discuss your answers with your mentor!

- Explain why "needs based" ministries are not adequate or complete ways to share the gospel message.

- The gospel message is good news about _____?

- What are the 4 main parts of a complete gospel presentation?

- Why is it important that unsaved people know a biblical definition of God before they hear the entire gospel message?

- What 3 things about God do they specifically need to know?

- What does an unsaved person need to know about their own condition before God?

- Explain how this helps them to see the need for God's salvation?

- What did Jesus do to provide a solution to man's separation from God?

- How does a person receive the benefits of Jesus' salvation?

- Why does God accept Jesus' life, death, and resurrection on behalf of sinful people?

- Explain why an intellectual acceptance of the facts regarding God, man, and Jesus are not sufficient to save a person.

> **SCRIPTURE MEMORIZATION**
> *For I am not ashamed of the gospel, for it is the power of God for salvation to everyone who believes, to the Jew first and also to the Greek.*
> **Romans 1:16**

SECTION 9

What Next?

If you've completed the entire Elder Training Handbook – congratulations! You've taken the first step toward becoming an Elder in your local church. Yes – I said *first step*. This handbook is not designed to be a "foolproof" way for your church leaders to find and appoint men for the role of Elder, it's designed to be a tool to help them in that process. How the rest of the process proceeds from here, is up to them.

They will need to determine what is next for you, in terms of further evaluation, congregational input, and other things. I've strongly suggested that they use a process similar to the one I outlined in the Introduction of this handbook, but they are free to progress any way they see fit. You should talk about "what's next" with the mentor who walked with you through the contents of this handbook.

But before you do that, let me say this. I'm very excited that you've made it this far. In my experience, not every man who begins this training finishes it. Some look over the handbook briefly and decide right then that it's more than they are willing to tackle! But you've made it. You've completed a very long, in-depth examination of yourself and the biblical role of Elder. Take a moment to thank the Lord for His grace in seeing you through.

Thank you for taking the time to invest in the Lord's work in His church, and in His work in you! Should you move on to serve as an Elder in your local church, you now have a strong foundation upon which to build... and you **should** continue to build!

As an Elder you will undoubtedly run into situations and circumstances that I have not covered in this handbook. You will need the wisdom of God's word and the help of your fellow Elders to face them wisely. I pray God's greatest help to you as you endeavor to lead His bride to maturity and the demonstration of His glory.

I leave you with the final words Paul gave to the Elders in Ephesus...

Pay careful attention to yourselves and to all the flock, in which the Holy Spirit has made you overseers, to care for the church of God, which he obtained with his own blood. - **Acts 20:28**

SECTION 10

Resources

The resources in this section are in a "ready to use" format. Feel free to copy any forms or evaluations from this section despite what copyright notices in the front of the handbook may say!

    A. Oral Theology Questionnaire Study Guide- - - - -p. 136
    B. Self-Evaluation form - - - - - - -p. 138
    C. Spousal Evaluation form - - - - - - -p. 144
    D. Pastoral Evaluation form - - - - - -p. 151
    E. Elder Team Evaluation Check-list - - - - -p. 157
    F. Meet N Greet Questions - - - - - -p. 163
    G. Congregational Evaluation Packets - - - -p. 165

Elder Oral Theology Questionnaire

In preparing for this oral exam, you will do well not only to know the answers to the points below, but also to know scriptures that relate to them. You want your confidence and strength in these issues to come from God's word. You will be allowed to use your Bible, but no notes, other than what is written in the margins of your Bible.

The Gospel
- What is the gospel?
- What 3 things does a person need to understand about God in order to fully grasp the gospel message?
- What 3 things do they need to understand about themselves?
- What 3 things do they need to understand about Jesus?
- What should they do to receive forgiveness from God?
- How would you personally explain to a person how they can become a Christian?

    SUGGESTED SCRIPTURES: Acts 17:22-35, Romans 3:23, 6:23, 5:6-8, 10:9-10, Ephesians 2:8-9, 1 Timothy 2:5, 1 Peter 3:18, John. 1:12, 1 Johnn. 5:12-13

The Trinity
- Where in the Bible are we taught about the Trinity?
- Explain what is meant by "Trinity."
- What is the significance of God being Trinity?
- Where in the Bible are we taught about Jesus' divine nature?
- Where in the Bible are we taught that the Holy Spirit is divine?
- Why is it vital that Jesus had both a divine and human nature?

    SUGGESTED SCRIPTURES: Genesis 1:1-3, Matthew 28:19, Mark 1:10-11, John 1:1-2:14, John 5:18, John 19:7, John 8:58, John 10:30, Acts 5:3-4, 2 Corinthians 13:14, Philippians 2:6-7, Colossians 2:9, Hebrews 2:14-18, Hebrews 9:14

Jesus
- Why did Jesus come to the earth?
- Why does it matter that He was without sin?
- What benefit do we receive from His substitutionary life, death, and resurrection?
- What is Jesus' role in our lives now?

    SUGGESTED SCRIPTURES: Matthew 4, John 3:16-18, Romans 3:22-26, Romans 5:7-21, Hebrews 2:18, Hebrews 4:15, Hebrews 9:24

RESOURCES

Holy Spirit
- What is the role of the Holy Spirit?
- List and explain some scriptures that show us what the Holy Spirit does in our salvation and in our sanctification.

    SUGGESTED SCRIPTURES: John. 14:15-26, John 16:7-13, Romans 8:16, 1 Corinthians 12:1-7,11, Ephesians 3:16

Scripture
- Explain what is meant by the Bible begin "inspired."
- What do the words "verbal, plenary" mean when speaking of inspiration of scripture?
- What do we mean when we say the Bible is "inerrant?"
- What do we mean when we say the Bible is "sufficient?"
- Explain why the Bibles we have today are trustworthy, even though we don't have any original copies of the scriptures?
- What is the role of scripture in our lives?

    SUGGESTED SCRIPTURES: Psalm 119, Proverbs 30:5, Isaiah 55:10-11, John 8:31, John 14:23, 2 Timothy 3:16, Hebrews 4:12, 2 Peter 1:21

Elder Candidate Self Evaluation Form

As a man considers the role of Elder as a possible ministry calling for his life, he is endeavoring to take on a task of great importance. He is stepping into a degree of ministry care and oversight that he's likely not been involved in previously on a regular basis. Please read each section carefully and respond as honestly as you are able. It is important for your sake and for the sake of the church family that you are as open and real about your strengths and weaknesses in each area as you can be. This will help everyone involved in the evaluation process have a better picture of your possible fit in the role of Elder.

PERSONAL MINDSET

- Explain how you understand the Elder to function within the church. What is his role and main priority?

- How do you feel about taking on the job of "co-shepherding," alongside the Pastor? Do you feel able to warmly connect with those within the church and express concern and care for them as they have need? Please elaborate…

RESOURCES

- Do you feel capable of confidently inquiring about the spiritual life, family health, life situation of those you may be assigned to touch base with? Please explain...

- How do you see yourself being an encouragement to those you lead in this way?

BIBLICAL QUALIFICATIONS

In each of the areas listed, please rank yourself on the 1 to 10 scale. In the space provided please explain why you ranked yourself as high or low as you did. Remember to rate yourself according to how things are in your life NOW, not how you would like them to be or what you are shooting for.

An Elder must be…

> **above reproach**

> Comments:

disciplined

Comments:

self-controlled

Comments:

respectable

Comments:

hospitable

Comments:

a man who is not a drunkard

Comments:

RESOURCES

gentle

Comments:

a man who is not quarrelsome

Comments:

a man who is not a lover of money or greedy for gain

Comments:

upright

Comments:

one who desires to be an Elder

Comments:

able to teach

Comments:

able to hold firmly to the trustworthy word

Comments:

able to instruct in sound doctrine

Comments:

able to rebuke those who teach bad doctrine

Comments:

be the husband of one wife,

Comments:

RESOURCES

one who has children who are believing

Comments:

one who has children who are obedient

Comments:

one who manages his own household well

Comments:

one who is not a new convert

Comments:

one who has a good reputation with those outside the church

Comments:

Name _____ Date _____

Signature_____

Spousal Evaluation

As a man considers the role of Elder as a possible ministry calling for his life, he is endeavoring to take on a task of great importance. He is stepping into a degree of ministry care and oversight that he's most likely not been involved in previously on a regular basis. In determining which men are ready for the challenge of Eldership and which men are not, we must do some in-depth evaluation...which includes the consideration of those closest to him. Naturally that includes you as his wife.

Each Elder candidate understands that their spouse will be asked some very direct and probing questions as part of the evaluation process. Each man has welcomed this opportunity. Please take the time to complete the following evaluation with these things in mind...

The role of Elder is one of high calling and responsibility. These men will be the ones who the church family trusts to hear from the Lord, follow His lead, and teach and direct the family in doing so. They are men who are called to set an example, guide the flock in godly wisdom, guard the church from doctrinal error, and set the pace and direction for the church and its ministries. It is vital that the right men, God's men, are in this role.

You are able to judge your husband's weaknesses and strengths from a standpoint that no other person can. Please be as honest as possible as your respond, as your answers will weigh heavily in the consideration of your husband for this position. If a response you give eventually leads your husband out of the Elder role, that will be a blessing to him, your family, and the church family. If he is not ready for the role, the weight of it would be far too great for him, and your family to bear.

Please understand that there is no sense in which these evaluations are meant to be overly strict or negatively judgmental. They are solicited with a desire to take the health of Jesus' church seriously by ensuring that the right men are discovered, and eventually accepted as the Elders of Community Church. In completing this evaluation, please do so prayerfully, free from your husband's input.

Thank you for your time and the willingness you have to share your husband with the church in a more official and significant way.

- Do you believe that your husband is wired in such a way that he is able to "co-shepherd," the church family alongside the Pastor?

RESOURCES

- Do you feel he is able to warmly connect with those within the church and express concern and care for them as they have need? Please elaborate...

- Do you think your husband is capable of confidently inquiring about a person's spiritual life, family health, and life situations with concern, compassion, and spiritual insight? Please explain...

- How do you see your husband being an encouragement to those he leads in this way?

- Do you feel like YOU and your family are ready for your husband to take on this added level of commitment and leadership at this time?

BIBLICAL QUALIFICATIONS

In each of the areas listed, please "rank" your husband on the 1 to 10 scale. In the space provided please explain why you ranked him as high or low as you did. Remember to rate him according to how things are in his life NOW, not how he's been in the past or how you hope he will be in the future.

An Elder must be…

    above reproach

    Comments:

    disciplined

    Comments:

RESOURCES

self-controlled

Comments:

respectable

Comments:

hospitable

Comments:

a man who is not a drunkard

Comments:

gentle

Comments:

a man who is not quarrelsome

Comments:

a man who is not a lover of money or greedy for gain

Comments:

upright

Comments:

one who desires to be an Elder

Comments:

able to teach

Comments:

RESOURCES

able to hold firmly to the trustworthy word

Comments:

able to instruct in sound doctrine

Comments:

able to rebuke those who teach bad doctrine

Comments:

be the husband of one wife,

Comments:

one who has children who are believing

Comments:

CAREY GREEN

one who has children who are obedient

Comments:

one who manages his own household well

Comments:

one who is not a new convert

Comments:

one who has a good reputation with those outside the church

Comments:

Name _____ Date _____

Signature_____

RESOURCES

Pastoral Evaluation

Individual Being Assessed _____ Date _____

PERSONAL MINDSET

- Does this man understand the role of Elder well?

- Do you feel he'd be a good co-shepherd, warmly, boldly, and compassionately dealing with people as needed?

- Do you feel he is capable of confidently inquiring about the spiritual life, family health, life situation of those he is assigned to touch base with?

- How do you feel about this man's fit with the current Elder team? Will there be a complementary "chemistry" with his addition?

BIBLICAL QUALIFICATIONS

An Elder must be...

    above reproach

        Comments:

    disciplined

        Comments:

    self-controlled

        Comments:

    respectable

        Comments:

RESOURCES

hospitable

Comments:

a man who is not a drunkard

Comments:

gentle

Comments:

a man who is not quarrelsome

Comments:

a man who is not a lover of money or greedy for gain

Comments:

upright

Comments:

one who desires to be an Elder

Comments:

able to teach

Comments:

able to hold firmly to the trustworthy word

Comments:

able to instruct in sound doctrine

Comments:

RESOURCES

able to rebuke those who teach bad doctrine

Comments:

be the husband of one wife,

Comments:

one who has children who are believing

Comments:

one who has children who are obedient

Comments:

one who manages his own household well

Comments:

CAREY GREEN

one who is not a new convert

Comments:

one who has a good reputation with those outside the church

Comments:

Name _____ Date _____

Signature_____

RESOURCES

Elder Team Evaluation Check List

Questions asked during interview, w/responses:

biblical Qualifications

An Elder must be…

    above reproach

        Comments:

    disciplined

        Comments:

    self-controlled

        Comments:

    respectable

        Comments:

RESOURCES

hospitable

Comments:

a man who is not a drunkard

Comments:

gentle

Comments:

a man who is not quarrelsome

Comments:

a man who is not a lover of money or greedy for gain

Comments:

upright

Comments:

one who desires to be an Elder

Comments:

able to teach

Comments:

able to hold firmly to the trustworthy word

Comments:

able to instruct in sound doctrine

Comments:

RESOURCES

able to rebuke those who teach bad doctrine

Comments:

the husband of one wife,

Comments:

one who has children who are believing

Comments:

one who has children who are obedient

Comments:

one who manages his own household well

Comments:

CAREY GREEN

one who is not a new convert

Comments:

one who has a good reputation with those outside the church

Comments:

Name _____ Date _____

Signature_____

RESOURCES

Elder Meet-n-Greet Suggested Questions

- Where did you grow up?
- How many siblings do you have?
- What was life like growing up?
- Did you grow up in Christian family?
- When did you accept Christ as your Lord and Savior?
- What times of testing have you had in your walk with Christ?
- What are some of the greatest lessons the Lord has taught you?
- Describe your devotional life.
- What has been your greatest joy? Your greatest heartache?
- What passages of scripture are your favorites?
- How does your Christian faith impact the way you see your vocation?
- Why do you desire to be an Elder?
- What do you bring to the Elder team?
- In what ways do you see your leadership as an Elder benefiting the church family?

Qualifications of an Elder
- Titus 1:5-9, 1 Timothy 3:1-7

Duties of an Elder
In the Bible, the distinction is made between a shepherd and a hired hand (*John 10:11-15*). A shepherd (elder) has in his heart a God-given love for the sheep and a desire to care for those entrusted to him. The hired hand is unwilling to become as emotionally involved - unwilling to confront the dangers that threaten the sheep - unwilling to truly love the people under his care.

As you consider a man for the position of elder, evaluate him in light of these six essential duties which characterize a good shepherd:

1. **Pastoral intimacy**
   An elder must be able to develop the relationships that under-gird all other ministry toward individual members.
   (John 10:11, 14)

2. **Pastoral tutelage**
   An elder must be able to provide personal biblical instruction for increasing character, skills, knowledge, faith, love, and enthusiasm among those under his care.
   (Acts 20:20, 27; 1 Timothy 4:16; 2 Timothy 3:16-17; 4:1-2 Titus 3:1-2, 8)

3. **Pastoral guidance**
   An elder must be able to offer objective biblical direction through conflicts, reversals of

life, distortions in thinking, and difficult decisions for those under his care.
(2 Timothy 3:16-17)

4. **Pastoral consolation**
   An elder must be able to give spiritual comfort to other believers during trials.
   (2 Corinthians 1:3-7; Thessalonians 5:14)

5. **Pastoral guardianship**
   An elder must be able to watch out for the enemy's assaults on the weakness of the sheep. He must warn the sheep of danger and discipline them when they become rebellious.
   (Acts 20:28-31; 1 Thessalonians 5:14; 1 Timothy 6:20; 2 Timothy 4:1-5; Hebrews 13:17)

6. **Pastoral intercession**
   An elder must pray with and for those entrusted to his care.
   (1 Samuel 12:23; Romans 1:9; Ephesians 1:15-21; Philippians 1:9-11; Colossians 1:9-12)

RESOURCES

Congregational Elder Evaluation

Name of Candidate:_____

SECTION 1: Who Can participate and how should they do so?

In order to participate in the evaluation and affirmation of Elders for our church family, you must meet the following requirements:

1. You are a recognized member the church, in good standing.
2. You are willing to submit your name (clearly legible) with your evaluation
3. You are willing to discuss any negative responses you give with the Elder Team - and potentially with the person you are evaluating.
4. Your evaluation is due to the Elder Team no later than _____.
5. **ONLY** return your evaluation to a member of the Elder Team or the church office.

SECTION 2: The Evaluation

As you complete the following evaluation, please do so:
- According to the descriptions on the attached pages.
- As honestly as you know how. (Concerns you may have will help us determine God's will)
- Only in areas where you have knowledge of the man in question. (If you come to a character trait that you honestly do not know about, leave it blank. We'd rather have sparse, but accurate information than plentiful but wrong information)

In this section, using the 1 to 10 scale, please indicate your impression of _____, as well as you are able. If any of your scores are 5 or less, please note why you scored the candidate the way you did in the "Comments" section under the question.

CAREY GREEN

An Elder must be…

    above reproach

        Comments:

    disciplined

        Comments:

    self-controlled

        Comments:

    respectable

        Comments:

    hospitable

        Comments:

RESOURCES

a man who is not a drunkard

Comments:

gentle

Comments:

a man who is not quarrelsome

Comments:

a man who is not a lover of money or greedy for gain

Comments:

upright

Comments:

one who desires to be an Elder

Comments:

able to teach

Comments:

able to hold firmly to the trustworthy word

Comments:

able to instruct in sound doctrine

Comments:

able to rebuke those who teach bad doctrine

Comments:

RESOURCES

the husband of one wife,

Comments:

one whose children are believing

Comments:

one who has children who are obedient

Comments:

one who manages his own household well

Comments:

one who is not a new convert

Comments:

CAREY GREEN

a man who has a good reputation with those outside the church

Thank you for the time and prayer you have invested in this vital step in the life of our church community. Please return your evaluation to any member of the Elder team or the church office.

PRINTED NAME _____

SIGNATURE _____

DATE: _____

A SPECIAL OFFER FOR OWNERS OF THIS BOOK!

The author is available to provide customized ON-SIGHT training for those who would like a deeper dive into the contents of this book — **at a special discounted price.**

POSSIBLE SCENARIOS FOR ON-SIGHT TRAINING:

- An existing Pastor or Elder team, seeking a deeper understanding of Biblical Eldership.
- A church-wide workshop to help congregations understand the Elder role and develop their own identification, assessment, and evaluation process.
- Training for a new cohort of potential Elders (a quick-start to the process).

DETAILS OF THIS OFFER:

- Contact the author to let him know you are interested in on-sight training.
- Explain your situation and provide a couple of desired dates for a training.
- Training can be one on one or group settings (the more, the merrier)
- You will ONLY be asked to pay for the author's travel and lodging expenses.
- Additional honorarium will be left up to your prayerful discretion.

TO TAKE THE NEXT STEP

Contact the author at Carey@CareyGreen.com

If you've found this book helpful, please leave a review of it on Amazon at https://CareyGreen.com/ETA-Review

Watch for these additional titles from Christian Home and Family
www.CareyGreen.com/Books

The Marriage Improvement Project (a devotional for couples)

The Dragon Slayer Chronicles (a fiction trilogy)

The Great Smizzmozzel Bash (a children's picture book)

Moving Toward God (19 discipleship lessons for new believers)

Recharge (Bible study methods and mindsets)

Podcasts by the author

THE MORNING MINDSET DAILY CHRISTIAN DEVOTIONAL

Over 70,000 daily downloads of the Morning Mindset demonstrate how this 6-minute mindset reset helps you get started for the day. Join us to get your mind aligned with the truth of God, from the scriptures, every single morning! Episodes are drawn directly from scripture, life-application-based, and challenging to mature and beginning Christ-followers alike. Find out more at https://CareyGreen.com or become a monthly partner and get access to our Partners-only podcast feed of bonus material at https://CareyGreen.com/Support

GOD FEARING KIDS AND THE PARENTS WHO RAISE THEM

If you are a Christ-follower and you have kids... then you intuitively know that you've got a massive job on your hands. It's one of the most amazing privileges given to human beings.

You get to fashion human beings into God-saturated, Christ-following, Kingdom-building individuals who make a difference in eternity... and all to the glory and praise of their Creator. That's not an easy job. We're here to help. Episodes are conversations about Christian parenting between retired Pastor, Carey Green and his wife of over 33 years, Mindi. They'll discuss what the Bible reveals about raising your children in a way that honors God and connects the child of your heart to the child of God. https://GodFearingKids.com

About the Author

Carey Green has been blessed to be in Christian ministry since 1988 when he began his first youth internship while attending Colorado Christian University. During those years he has served the church in a variety of areas including youth ministry, worship, administration, small group coordination, associate pastor, and lead or senior pastor.

He has been married since 1989 to his best friend and ministry partner Mindi and has 5 children.

With over 20 years of ministry experience, Carey is available to consult on the topics in this book and many others.

Carey is also the host of the Morning Mindset Daily Christian Devotional podcast. A daily, 6-minute mindset reset that helps a worldwide audience get their minds aligned with the truth of God's word daily. Find out more about the MM at https://CareyGreen.com

Carey and his wife have also founded the non-profit – Not A Needy Person – which enables Christ-followers to submit needs, have them vetted and presented to the audience – and met by other Christ-followers. Find out more at http://NotANeedyPerson.com.

Made in the USA
Middletown, DE
05 February 2024

49104758R00110